The

Jerk Whisperer

*How to deal with tyrants, tormentors,
and bullies...and still keep your sanity!*

To Lauren,
Thanks for all your support
best wishes —
Steve

by Dr. Stephen Birchak, Ed.D.

Royal Fireworks Press
Unionville, New York

*"We can train ourselves to wake up every day and
tell ourselves: there will be no crises today. It's that
simple. Most crises are in our heads, not in the real
world. When you remove the imaginary crises from
your life, you will find that you have a lot more time to
give away your smiles, give away your hugs, see
the best in others, solve problems, and relieve
a little bit of the suffering in the world."*

Nick Birchak
1984-2011

Son, and friend. Lover of life and laughter.
He gave away all his smiles. He danced to every song.
The world became a better place because of his years in it.
This book is dedicated to his memory.

Royal Fireworks Press
First Avenue, PO Box 399
Unionville, NY 10988-0399
(845) 726-4444
FAX: (845) 726-3824
email: mail@rfwp.com
website: rfwp.com

ISBN: 978-0-89824-372-7

Printed and bound in the United States of America using vegetable-based
inks on acid-free, recycled paper and environmentally friendly cover coat-
ings by the Royal Fireworks Printing Co. of Unionville, New York.

Table of Contents

It has become appallingly clear that our technology has surpassed our humanity. I hope that someday, our humanity might yet surpass our technology.

—*Albert Einstein*

Definition of *jerk*: A fool; a stupid person

Definition of *whisperer*: One who speaks very softly without vibration of the vocal cords

Introduction

As you begin to read this book, it is important to reflect on where you stand in regard to your goals in your relationships with your fellow human beings.

If you want to know how to put jerks and idiots or jackasses in their place, stop now and look for another book (perhaps in the "How to Increase Anger" section of the bookstore).

If you want to get even with the hostile people in your life, please ask for your money back and enroll in an Ultimate Fighting training course.

If you are looking for skills to dominate others, you are wasting your time reading the wrong book.

However, if you are interested in discovering insights into your life, reducing your stress, cultivating love, and promoting human compassion, you are in the right place. The goal of this book is not to beat down the jerks, but to help them (and help ourselves) to find the courage that guides us to kindness, gentleness, and peacefulness.

The reason that jerks are jerks is because they see the world as a hostile place, and they see it as their job and their right to be abusive and aggressive.

The Jerk Whisperer is a guide for average people with average struggles. It is a book for those who possess an unwavering desire to make the world a better place. If you want to understand how you react to hostility, how you get stuck, how you can change your thinking, and ultimately create new behaviors to influence and elevate the people around you, then you are in the right place.

> Only one thing makes a dream impossible: the fear of failure.
>
> —*Paulo Coelho*

This pursuit may be the most difficult undertaking in your life. Often, when we pursue our goals in life, we struggle when we meet failure. It's natural to lose a little hope when we fail, but if you've chosen to deal with the hostility in the world, you should never hesitate or stop because you are frustrated. Nor should you stop because you may believe that you don't have all the tools for dealing with all of the aggression in the world. You don't need a Ph.D. to improve the world. You don't need money, fame, or success to make a difference. If you really want something different in your life, don't wait until you feel like you have a huge set of skills or qualifications. Most of the things we follow with our heart don't require wealth, extraordinary education, or a high IQ, because most of the things we follow with our heart only require a gracious determination and a genuine will to make a difference in the world.

There are two major reasons why we fail in our quests in life. First, we are afraid to fail, and this can keep us from starting, and often we use this as an excuse to quit and join the cynics. Been there....Tried that....Done that....Why should I care?

Second, we sell ourselves short because we see ourselves as average people incapable of making a difference. All great causes are pursued with fear and self-doubt, but fear and self-doubt only have power over us if we see them as a wall instead of mere bumps in the road. All great causes became triumphs because average people were able to move forward with a trembling heart and extraordinary commitment.

The essence of this book is to help average people accomplish the task of promoting harmony in their lives. In the end, it's worth the struggle to become a skilled Jerk Whisperer. Don't be afraid of a trembling heart, because with each effort, you will find your heart beating stronger. Mostly, remember that kindness, compassion, and love are infinitely more joyful than anger, aggression, and hostility. Simply, life is much more fun as a Jerk Whisperer than as a jerk.

Step One:

Prepare Yourself for Change

Psychological diagnosis?
Is it PTSD? ADHD? OCD? No…it's JPN
Jerks can be JPN (just plain nuts!),
but the prognosis is promising.

The car rolled forward and stopped next to the drive-up mailbox at the post office. The driver was an elderly woman named Margaret, affectionately known to her friends, loved ones, and grandchildren as "Grandma Mickey."

This was one stop among many for her that day. She was dropping off a stack of letters and cards at the drive-up mailbox at the post office. Grandma Mickey mails a lot of letters and cards—it's what sweet grandmas do. She took an extra moment that day because she had so many things to mail and she wanted to check each letter to be certain she put a stamp on each one.

Suddenly there was a fist pounding on the window of her car. A frantic middle-aged woman screamed from the other side of the glass as her fist continued to pound. In that moment, Grandma Mickey nearly jumped out of her seat. She rolled down the window in order to hear the woman and perhaps respond to her emergency.

"Hey Lady! This is a quick stop! Not a rest stop! Move your damn car!"

Dave dialed up his favorite website for book sales. He was excited to see how his new book was doing. He had spent the last three years of his life writing a book about how couples can improve their relationships. When he viewed the information on his book, he was surprised to see a critique that described it as "...ridiculous...a waste of time...condescending." Dave was confused how anyone could write such a description about a book that was designed to help people reflect on love, compassion, and kindness. Later, David discovered that the critique had been submitted by a jealous colleague.

Steve pumped the brakes on his car as he noticed the stoplight ahead turning yellow. Suddenly, a large red SUV flew into his lane, passed him, and swerved into the empty road between Steve and the stoplight. The SUV missed his front fender by mere inches. Steve slammed on his brakes to avoid a collision. With his heart pounding, he gave a quick honk of the horn, unsure if the SUV driver had seen him. As the light turned, the SUV crept forward a few feet then abruptly stopped. The stop-and-go of the SUV happened three more times, and now the driver was honking his horn and flailing his left arm out the window, giving the finger to Steve behind him. Steve finally decided simply to change lanes and drift back; it was his habit to try to avoid reckless drivers whenever possible. The red SUV slowed in the other lane until the two cars were side by side. The SUV driver then honked several times and swerved toward him. At the next light, the two cars stopped side by side again. The honking continued, and Steve glanced to his left to see the passenger window rolling down. Suddenly, a loud bang came from Steve's car door, followed by the screeching of tires as the SUV ran through the red light and sped away. Steve opened his car door to see a long window scraper lying on the ground. The SUV driver had thrown the ice scraper before driving away.

♦ ♦ ♦

These three scenes are real, everyday occurrences, and they are not uncommon. We see and hear jerks in traffic, stores, malls, workplaces, and neighborhoods. The first scene happened to my dear mother, Grandma Mickey. If you asked all of her grandchildren, "Who is the sweetest person on earth?" All of them would most certainly reply, "Grandma Mickey." Did she deserve the wrath of the jerk pounding on her window?

The second scene happened to a friend. His anonymous critique was all too common. Kids do it to each other. They diss one another by making comments behind their backs—behind the safe cloak of the Internet. (*Diss* is the slang term for the act of making disparaging remarks about someone.) In the case of Dave, his colleague was an adolescent trapped in an adult body. In the age of technology, accountability is not a prerequisite to having an opinion.

The third scene happened to me. That particular morning I was driving to the college where I teach counseling psychology courses. After the SUV sped away, I reached out my car door and scooped up the ice scraper. As I drove closer to the college I had to circle the block a few times while seeking a parking spot, and to my astonishment, I spotted the SUV and its crazy driver as he parked in front of an apartment, turned off his engine, and walked indoors.

I took the ice scraper to my developmental psychology class that day and passed it around to all the students as I described the incident. I also shared with them that I knew where this SUV was currently located. I asked my students to write down and discuss the most inappropriate ways that they could deal with this incident. I was quite proud that I had so many creative students in my class. The inappropriate solutions generated a great deal of laughter. Some of the more entertaining ideas included, "How about if you jammed it into his tail pipe and left a note? …No, I have a better idea! Send it in the mail with a note saying, 'Forget something?'…Here's a better idea! What if you simply wrapped it up in a bow with a sweet letter letting him know that you are watching him? …Oh no! Your best move would be to crazy glue the ice scraper to the hood of his car!"

I also shared the story of Grandma Mickey, and of course, my students had just as many creative ideas about how we could have dealt with that woman, too. It was a lively class discussion that day. We talked about civility, conscience, aggression, and how these issues affect us in everyday life. There was one insight that all of the students agreed upon. When we are subjected to meanness, it is easier to think of revenge than it is to let it go. In other words, it is quite common to obsess on getting even when we are mistreated. My graduate students also agreed that they would not act on those impulses to retaliate. We discussed the implications of moral development in a society that glorifies and values retaliation, power, and intimidation.

As a group, the students also concluded that revenge would only escalate the problem. We discussed another recent incident of a cat and mouse road rage episode. It ended with a middle-age affluent woman pulling out a gun, walking up to a car, and murdering the person she believed had violated her. Other students told stories of neighbors retaliating, shoppers attacking other shoppers, and examples of average people lashing out at those whom they claimed were the most important in their lives—their loved ones. In all cases, we recognized and feared these moments of a loss of personal control. And while we can reverse the trend, in many cases, we do things to one another that can't be repaired.

In the end, we are left shaking our heads and shaking in our shoes. It's easy to think about giving my pain to my perpetrator but a lot harder to seek peaceful solutions. We need solutions, and we need a philosophy for dealing with aggression. And the most frightening reality is that we often are unable to see the aggression in ourselves. Many polls and studies have revealed that most people believe the majority of people in this world are rude, but only a small percentage place themselves in that category. We are much quicker to accuse others of their rudeness than we are to recognize it in ourselves.

I've spoken to large groups of people, and I often will ask them to raise their hands if they are confessed "road ragers." In an audience of five hundred people, only three or four will raise their hands. I then share the research indicating that around 50% of all people driving on the road will respond to other drivers with aggression when they are confronted with aggression. We are slow to admit the wrongdoer within but quick to recognize it in others.

I have a wonderful friend who works in a high-stress job with high-stress people, and she often seeks my advice on how to deal with the jerks in her life. After one of our discussions, she said, "You are so important in my life in the ways that you help me to think about these jerks."

I replied, "Yes, I'm just a regular Jerk Whisperer." We laughed for several minutes at the idea of being a Jerk Whisperer. I've watched many programs that feature people who work with animals and have tremendous talents dealing with their behaviors, but in all of those cases, it's a little easier than dealing with humans. Humans are not horses. You can't throw a lasso around the hooves of your irate boss, hold him down, and get him to succumb to cooperation. Humans are not dogs. You can't put a collar on the guy standing next to you in the store and jolt it until he obeys and "knows who's in charge." You can't pull a driver out of her car, pin her to the ground, and hold her until she submits to appropriate behavior.

We're not dealing with animals; we are dealing with people, and we need to construct our approach carefully. We need to understand who they are, the impact they have on us, and what will work best (for us and them) if we expect a positive outcome.

I speak to thousands of people every year about how we treat one another. I speak to auditoriums full of students about bullying and how it destroys lives. I make presentations to teachers and administrators about how to shape character—by starting with themselves. I talk to parent groups about love and self-discipline. I talk to colleges, corporations, businesses, and organizations about relationships as the key to productivity. One of my most favorite times, however, is after I speak. People talk to me about hope and love. They talk about kindness, helpfulness, patience, and the power of human decency.

Every time I talk to someone about incivility, it's impossible to avoid the emotional toll: we are afraid. One thing is abundantly clear: there is a lot of pain in this world. We can be very cruel to one another and can inflict a lot of pain. In children, bullying is increasing. In adults, rageful behavior has become normative. Studies have shown that 50% of us have been bullied on the job. Fear of terrorism, random shootings, and rageful conduct have resulted in a shift in the way we see one another and in how much we trust one another. The saddest testimony to our pain is how our personal sorrow has reached tragic proportions. According to the World Health Organization, suicide rates have increased by more than 60% in the last half-century.

> The instant you have lost hope in tomorrow is the instant you lose meaning for today.
> —Mike Hutchison

Despite all of this, when I speak to others about civility, I see smiles; I get handshakes and sometimes hugs. There is also hope, faith, and a lot of joy. Many people are stopping, listening, and thinking about what is going on. The exciting phenomenon is this: we want to talk and think about these issues, and there are many people who are starting to believe that we can change the world by changing ourselves.

I have listened, and it is clear that many of us have created unfounded beliefs about our fears. I also talk with people about how these fears may escalate human tension and negatively affect motivation. We need to start with some of the most common views and consider how we have swallowed these beliefs as though they are truths that apply to everyone.

Some of the things I hear people say are:

• Jerks are everywhere! They make us crazy!

• They ruin our lives, raise our stress levels, and they are unstoppable!

• The world is going downhill fast, and we need to stop these jerks!

• The world is becoming a hopeless place because of them!

• It's important to put up a good fight because if we don't, it will result in jerks running the world!

When we espouse our views on how to deal with the aggression in the world, we have to decide whether we want to light another fuse under the powder kegs or smother the ones that have been lit. If our views result in an increase in aggression, we have chosen to detonate the bombs within ourselves and others. We have chosen to make the world a more volatile place. In order to smother the sizzling fuse, we need to take a deep breath and examine our beliefs about aggressive people, as well as confront the antagonism in ourselves. Most people recognize that many of our beliefs are, for the most part, not only unproductive, but also a quick reaction to serious problems. Every one of the previous statements are not true, but we hear them everyday.

If you have ever heard yourself making any of those statements, you may need to adopt a more productive philosophy, and you need to strive to make yourself a Jerk Whisperer. In this negative picture, you present doom, gloom, apathy, and cynicism. When you buy into this negativity, you lose all your power and all your potential. Additionally, you allow the aggression in the world to have control over you. Is that what you want?

> Those who make peaceful revolution impossible will make violent revolution inevitable.
> —John F. Kennedy

Perhaps it's time to get our power back. How did we arrive at a place where hostility controls our thoughts, affects our well-being, and becomes a force we are ill-equipped to deal with?

Let's start with the first one: *"Jerks are everywhere."* This misconception materializes because we have become hypervigilant toward antagonistic behavior. It may seem like the jerks are everywhere, but they are not. The world is overwhelmingly filled with an abundance of compassionate and caring people, and it is my belief that the bullies are a very small minority (regardless of the culture, ethnicity, language, religion, country, or location). The fact is this: jerks cannot be in all places all the time. They pop up here and there, and when they do, if we are not careful, we start to think everyone we meet is a tyrant because we cannot stop thinking about them. In fact, the opposite is true: kind people are everywhere. Helpful people are everywhere. Loving and compassionate people take opportunities to help each other every day.

In this book, you will learn how to stop yourself when you see the world as a bad place; perhaps you will even see more of the good in the world.

> All blame is a waste of time. No matter how much fault you find with another, and regardless of how much you blame him, it will not change you.
>
> —*Wayne Dyer*

"They make us crazy!" They do not. When was the last time you asked a four-year-old, "Why did you hit him?" Often, the response is, "He made me hit him!" After you hear the child say this, you probably scold the child and say, "He can't make you hit him! You chose to hit him!" The same holds true for our relationships with aggressive people. "Aunt Patty makes me crazy!" No, you choose to be crazy when Aunt Patty is neurotic.

There are certain people in this world to whom you react more strongly than others. After reading this book, you will learn how to identify which people tend to get under your skin more than others. You also will learn how to calm yourself when they do.

"They ruin our lives, raise our stress levels, and they are unstoppable!" There may be a correlation between your stress and the knucklehead standing next to you in line at the grocery store, but it doesn't mean he is causing it. The evidence is clear. There are people in your line who are not stressing in the presence of the jerk's behavior. The difference? One person gives up his power to the jerk, and one chooses not to. Aggressive people don't deserve to own your power; they are just people who act out! In this book, you will learn how to keep your power—forever.

> A pessimist sees the difficulty in every opportunity;
> an optimist sees the opportunity in every difficulty.
> —*Winston Churchill*

"The world is going downhill fast...." The world is becoming more crowded each day (in fact, as you read this, they are making more people out there), and it is changing with each passing minute. The problem is not the jerks; it's our inability to adapt to them or deal with them. The world is not going downhill; it is simply changing. The marvels of technology are easing more pain in the world than at any other time in the history of humankind. Cancer survival rates are at their highest, medications are curing more illnesses than ever before, and surgical procedures on our eyes, ears, and major organs are improving our lives in ways our ancestors never dreamed of! In many ways, the world is improving every day.

There are those who see the glass as half full, others who see it half empty, and we now have a new breed of humans who see it half full...of poison. This book will help you to pour the poisons out of your glass and fill it back up with life. There is an old saying: "Anger is like poisoning yourself and hoping the other person dies." Your time on earth is too short to be poisoning yourself.

"...and we need to stop these jerks!" If you spent your entire lifetime on a mission to stop jerks, there would still be plenty of jerks left over to inflict their misery on the rest of us. Jerks have been with us forever. I am sure at one time at the dawn of humankind there were plenty of cave jerks who delighted in dousing other's fires—just because they could. There was probably a guy who tossed and turned under his animal skin as his spouse asked, "Why can't you sleep?" to which he promptly replied, "Aw, I just can't stop thinking about caveman

Bob. He's always stomping out everyone's fires! I'd like to give him a cave beat-down, but I have a reputation as a cave gentleman, and I don't know what to do!"

We will never stop all the jerks in the world, but we can diminish their negative influence when we are willing to invest energy in helping them instead of executing them. This book will give you the skills to make a powerful difference.

> Most of the important things in this world have been accomplished by people who have kept on trying when there seemed to be no hope at all.
> —*Dale Carnegie*

"*The world is becoming a hopeless place because of them!*" The mere fact that you are reading this sentence right now is because of hope. You want something different. You want progress. You want to be enthusiastic for a solution and believe you are not alone. There is an abundance of hope in the world and a great number of people who believe that if we created this problem, we can dismantle it as well. This book will help you keep your hope alive, develop skills, and reduce those things that raise your stress level.

> A person who is nice to you but rude to the waiter is not a nice person.
> —*Dave Barry*

"It's important to put up a good fight because if we don't, it will result in jerks running the world!" In any fight, there has to be a loser. There is no such thing as a good fight. A fight, by its very nature, is an act of destruction. We will never create peace in the world with fanaticism, a bomb, or a gun. We create peace with education, literacy, schools, equal rights for women worldwide, respect for cultural differences, and the genuine desire to take a stance against oppression. There are good resolutions to conflicts, but there are no good fights. There is always a better solution than destruction. On rare occasions, we may need force for defense and protection, but it doesn't work as an educational tool. We don't want to make it our goal to annihilate and demolish anyone who crosses us. We want to be good peacemakers and negotiators and develop long-lasting, productive relationships. A good Jerk Whisperer wants both parties to win and to emerge from the other side as better human beings. One of the reasons why tension and hostility exist is because peace is not enough for many people these days. Rather than "live and let live," we practice "cross me and you die." The "do unto others" has become a battle cry for revenge instead of living by the Golden Rule of treating others as we wish to be treated.

The jerks are not running the world; they simply are disrupting it. We have to make sure that their disruptions do not keep us from the beauty and the potential that exist in the world. In this book, you will learn how to be at peace with some of the injustices and put energy into the issues that matter.

> Our happiness depends on the habit of mind we cultivate. So practice happy thinking every day. Cultivate the merry heart, develop the happiness habit, and life will become a continual feast.
> —*Norman Vincent Peale*

We start with what we cultivate

Many years ago at a meeting, I worked with an individual who proclaimed, "Those damn secretaries never do anything for me!" (This person was an angry, self-persecuting jerk. In Step Two, we will examine the various types of jerks. The self-persecuting jerk believes he or she is always a victim.) I reported to my co-worker my belief that the secretaries were wonderful people and very helpful to me. At the heart of this situation was a simple truth: when we act like jerks, how can we expect anything different in return? Aggressive people often attribute their misery to the external world; therefore, they believe they are justified in their actions. This person, who was troubled by the secretaries, was clueless to the part she played in the exchange. She failed to see that the secretaries simply reflected aggression or kindness back. These particular secretaries worked well with anyone (male, female, short, tall, old, young, neurotic, or otherwise) who treated them with the decency and the dignity they deserved.

Life works this way. Our personal lives are like a series of continual plantings and re-plantings of crops. With each season, we need to deal with the changing variables. If we want growth, we need to plant continually through monsoons, droughts, and changing weather. If we do not pay attention to the inconsistencies, our lives are less effective. You cannot control the weather, but you can control the fertilizer. A fertile life is a well-tended life, and a fruitful life gets to have that "continual feast" that Norman Vincent Peale mentions in the quote on the previous page.

> I'd kill for a Nobel Peace Prize.
>
> —*Steven Wright*

As absurd as the quote on the previous page may sound, if we truly reflect on what comedian Steven Wright said, it is obvious that many people seem to engage in that kind of behavior every day. It is irrational to believe that violence can be used to create peace. If we truly believe in kindness, why do we try to beat respect into other human beings? Instead of fighting with the world, we need to figure out how to make ourselves promoters of harmony. The most influential and life-changing figures in the history of humankind always have focused their efforts on power *with* others instead of power *over* others. Hitler, Stalin, and a variety of other historical figures have sought to destroy others, have power *over* others, and control others. Mother Teresa, Gandhi, and Martin Luther King, Jr. sought to have power *with* others. Their goal was to make the world a better place. We make a lot of mistakes in our relationships with others, but the biggest mistake we make is when we seek to have complete control over situations or individuals. An excessive need to control others stems from insecurities, and unfortunately, the jerk believes control can only be obtained through the infliction of fear and aggression. Sadly, it becomes a horrible exercise in wasted energy.

In a world of tension, technology, and fast pace, we need to slow down and examine the variables affecting our everyday existence. No one will go to their grave wishing, "Gosh, I should have been more of a jerk; perhaps I should have been more anxious. By golly, I let too many people in my lane on the highway! I spent too much time hugging my loved ones! What was I thinking? If only I could have dominated and controlled more people...perhaps given them more pain...then my life would have had meaning. I would have had more money, and I would have finally been able to afford that 165 horsepower outboard motor and boat...."

In the end, we realize that the meaning in our life is measured not by what we acquired, but in how we elevated the lives of others. We need to start by rising above the insanity instead of joining it.

In this book, you will be able to create a series of insights that enable you to understand and deal with these situations. You will be able to answer several personal questions:

- What are my most common reactions to jerks?
- Who are these jerks anyway?
- How is this altering my life, my relationships, and my health?

You also become more aware of these people (instead of merely reacting to them). When you understand how they became who they are, it not only will allow you to become more effective in dealing with them, it also will allow you to inoculate your human spirit and maybe even develop immunity from their toxic lives.

Most importantly, after you understand aggressive people and your reactions to them, you can take a number of steps to alter outcomes and change your personal life forever. Cruelty can take its toll on many of us (myself included). It's time to stop paying that toll and save that pocket change for ourselves. All humans deserve peaceful lives. We deserve long, healthy, and productive lives. We can accomplish these things when we embrace the Jerk Whisperer way of life.

> He who smiles rather than rages is always the stronger.
>
> *—Japanese Proverb*

Letting go of insanity instead of letting it in

I have a dear friend named Lindy. We had not seen each other in quite a while, and she filled me in on a horrible divorce she had gone through. It was a challenging time in her life, and Lindy described how her former husband, Frank, hurt her through verbal and psychological abuse, followed by an attempt in court to paint a picture of her as a bad mother. Frank did everything in his power to say nasty, untrue things about Lindy. It was a self-centered effort to gain custody of their son. Lindy had raised her son, Nicky, all by herself for the past nine years. Frank was now reappearing and using every tactic available to defame her character. In the end, he failed to do this, but he put Lindy through a living hell and an extraordinary amount of pain. It was clear that it was one of the most difficult times of her life. When she had finished describing this heartbreaking scenario, she smiled and said, "Do you know what I really hope for?" For a minute, I thought, *I know what many people would hope for: a misguided bus in his track...perhaps a serious case of cramps while Frank was swimming...maybe he could be abducted in a foreign country while he is on his next cruise....*

However, this was Lindy. Lindy was a saint, a mother, and a decent human being. I was not surprised to hear her say, "I have hope that one day he will turn a corner and find peace. I think he has the potential. I really hope life turns out okay for him."

Her peaceful demeanor was not surprising. Lindy is one of the most joyful and caring people I have ever known. She wishes everyone well. She does not seek revenge; she lives by a principle that transcends an absolute right or wrong mentality. She seeks a long-term peace, and she does not waste any energy in wishing bad things. She only wants good things for a person who purposely inflicted pain upon her. To me, Lindy is an amazing human being. Her goal was to find serenity and wish it for him as well. She wanted to change her current situation, but her goal was so full of compassion that she was still wishing the best for others who hurt her. I have never forgotten that moment.

Lindy is one of my favorite normal-neurotic friends (I consider myself in this group as well. I am not only flawed like many of my normal-neurotic friends; I am profoundly flawed). Like many others, Lindy is less than perfect, stressed more than she needs to be, does not always sleep well, wishes she could be better with her diet, and on and on. She is a beautifully flawed human being. In spite of her struggles, her spirit makes the world a better place, and she is raising a delightful, loving son who also will make the world a better place.

Lindy's story reminds me of how we are often consumed with thoughts of hurting others when they hurt us. Lindy's goal was to regain her sanity. If she would have clung to cruel intentions, she most certainly would have moved further away from personal peace and sanity. We see examples of ill-thinking every day, and we see its destructive path. It does not take any courage, skill, or strength to pursue an aggressive path; in fact, aggression is generally an indicator that an individual has given up.

When was the last time you heard someone reciting his scrambled resentments toward life? We hear people rant, "Oh! What an awful, horrible, rotten, idiot my ex-husband is! And today marks the fourteenth anniversary since I divorced that awful, creepy, awful, hideous, awful, piece of garbage, no good... did I mention awful?"

When I hear people resenting others like this, I am tempted to ask, "Isn't it time to move on? Or at least put your energy into something productive?"

If we want to change our current situation (when we feel like we are losing our sanity), we need to ask ourselves, "Why do I want to deal with this in the first place? In other words, What is my long-term goal?" When we set goals, we bring structure to the chaos in our life. Psychological pain is often the result of seeking the wrong things in life. To deal effectively with others, we need to understand that sometimes the best learning takes place when we un-learn first.

As we get older, we often discover that life's greatest learning experiences take place not through what we take in, but in what we let go. We find out how much better off we will be if we let go of things rather than cling to them. There is an abundance of literature that seeks to deal with tough people, tough situations, and tough circumstances. Some of it has to do with power over others, getting even, paying someone back, putting someone in his place, or making sure others feel our pain. A Jerk Whisperer's starting point has to be to let go of painful habits and move the pain away rather than harbor it.

The first thing we need to do is to recognize the pain we may feel from being around aggressive people. The loss of personal power is a choice, not a life mandate. Miserable people believe they are condemned to life, but they are condemned to life only by their choices and their habits. Pain is often a part of life, but suffering is a choice.

If you have ever felt stressed from your interactions with jerks, be comforted in knowing that you do not have to feel this way. Changing your habits of thinking and behaving can have automatic results and an immediate surge in life satisfaction.

Step Two:

Understand Your Reaction to Jerks

Do jerks really make us crazy?

To address the question "Do jerks really make us crazy?" we need to begin by examining an impractical belief: *Other people cause my insanity.*

Behavioral psychology teaches us that life often can be reduced to stimulus and response. The behavioral approach assumes that life can be summed up similarly to the way in which we train an animal to react to its environment. Roll over and you get a biscuit! I have a problem with this line of thinking because, like many people, I am too stubborn. I believe there is a gap between the stimulus and the response, and this gap is called a choice. Many of us believe we have choices. However, some people believe in choices only when they are convenient. Others believe they never have a choice.

People in this last group always will be doomed to their thoughts. Many people believe they have choices and are free to enjoy life, but miserable people believe they are sentenced to life. They rarely see the joy in life because they only can obsess on the things they believe keep them from their personal happiness.

If you believe someone is causing your insanity, grab a mirror. It is, in fact, you who are insane.

Happy, productive, and well-adjusted people have a strong belief in the control they exercise in that gap between the stimulus and the response. They believe they have the power to choose how they want to react in a given set of circumstances. Your boss is not making you crazy; you have trained yourself to act crazy when your boss acts that way. The same holds true when you say, "Traffic, long lines, and my co-workers make me crazy." It is impossible for these things to make you crazy, and the secret is to seize as much of that gap between the stimulus in the world and how you react to it. Your choice will determine your response, and your response will organize, construct, and determine your future, your sanity, your health, and your joy.

When we believe that other people cause our reactions, we are volunteering to be a hostage to circumstances.

The six most common reactions to jerks

Most people have an aversion to being mistreated by a jerk. I am one of them. I truly detest mistreatment by a jerk, but there is something I often despise even more than being mistreated— my reaction to it.

Most people have a conscience. One of the qualities of having a conscience is that it forces you to reflect on your own behavior. If you have ever felt a knot in your stomach because you did not like the way you reacted toward someone, be comforted; this is actually a good sign of your character. The good news is this: if you did not like yourself, it is an internal indicator that you have a sense of right and wrong. Many jerks do not get that knot in their stomach because they have personality disorders. If you get that knot, you are merely a normal-neurotic. (For the record, I love my fellow normal-neurotics. We struggle together!)

Often we may deal with our unpleasant and disagreeable personal qualities by defending them or dressing them up in rationalizations. But no matter how we dress them up by saying to ourselves, "They had it coming... I needed to put them in their place... They needed to be punished... justice had to be served," in the end, it leaves us feeling empty and upset. It always comes full circle, and we end up looking in the mirror and saying, "I don't like myself when I act that way."

We like to seek answers to our problems, but in many cases, we do not solve a problem but displace it into something we believe we cannot control. If we cannot find the answer in our environment, we sometimes blame our past. If that does not work, we blame our own genetics. "I wasn't myself; it was the alcoholic... I've got my mother's temper... my father's impatience...."

In Step Three, we will examine myths and excuses in more detail, but if you feel guilt and if you have ever been disappointed with that person in the mirror, good! Do not change! You need that internal dialogue, and if you ever lose it, you are really in trouble.

It is easy to identify those who have lost this essential internal dialogue. They have lost their will to be a decent human being. They have lost their will to exercise kindness. They have joined the bitter and the apathetic. They have given up and given in. They have bowed to the pressures to enter the world of jerkdom, and now they have lost their freedom and their dignity. They see themselves as prisoners in the world of hostility.

If you struggle with these issues, it is a great sign that you are alive. If you have a hard time dealing with it, good! You have not given up, and you are still a vibrant member of a society of people who are concerned and motivated toward making the world a better place.

It is important to stay diligent in your efforts to change. If you ever find energy in your thoughts of ill will, you have entered a dangerous place. This is when you have stepped over the line into the world of hate.

For many people, if they did not have hate, they would have no energy at all. Haters use every tool possible to justify why they feel the way they do. Hate is fanaticism. You can hate in the name of politics, religion, or nationalism. However, no matter how you slice it, hate is hate, and it is destructive.

One of the keys to becoming a Jerk Whisperer is to be keenly aware of how the jerks affect you and to not adopt the habits you despise. We sometimes become so consumed with the people we despise that we end up developing hatred toward them. You're drifting toward a philosophy of hate if:

- You believe you are justified in mistreating others.
- You are obsessing at great lengths about how you wish they could feel your pain.
- You've given up your quest for comforting others and replaced it with a need to punish others.
- You take joy in others' misfortunes.

Hatred may appear in a brief moment on the highway or in the workplace, or it may be a habit of clinging to a desire to have others experience pain and unhappiness. If we could capture the energy that people expend toward their desire to have others feel their pain and redirect it toward a quest for joy (even if it is merely selfish personal joy), the result would be a planet that would become a paradise for humanity. It would not even matter if the energy was only selfishly directed toward one's own needs; at least it would eliminate the constant affliction of pain on others!

We need to start by examining our common reactions and determine which ones we regularly experience. The six major dysfunctional styles of reacting to jerks are:

- **The Defensive Lineman**
- **The Doormat**
- **The Simmering Stew**
- **The Commiserator**
- **The Defeated**
- **The Deer in the Headlights**

If we are these kinds of people with these reactions, we become prisoners to our thoughts. It is not a crime, and you are not insane if you have any of these reactions. I know of no human being who has not had some of them. Holocaust survivor Viktor Frankl once said, "An abnormal reaction to an abnormal situation is normal." These reactions may seem natural in some situations, but it is important to realize that if we continue to act in this way, we will continue to be miserable. These reactions are decisions. They are decisions with consequences.

We have to try to recognize if we have trained ourselves to relinquish our power to the jerks in our lives (something all of us realize is such a waste!). All irrational reactions have one thing in common: they are a waste of energy.

All human beings are susceptible to these reactions. They may differ from individual to individual. For some, it is a part-time behavior; for others, it is a daily state of misery.

There are two important reflective questions you should ask yourself: "Which reactions am I guilty of?" and "How often?" It's important to realize that whenever we have these reactions, we have given up. Sometimes it may be temporary, and sometimes it may be for longer durations of time. In all of the following examples, we may tell ourselves, "I hate it when I overreact to these people!" A good place to start changing is to stop using the term *overreact*.

If a person quickly grabbed the collar of a child and jerked him out of the way of an oncoming car, we would not say, "Gosh, you overreacted!" We would realize that the vigilant adult was ready to respond and acted on a quick impulse. When you are discontented with how you react to jerks, these are not over-reactions; these are styles or habits of relating. Dysfunctional habits of thinking result in emotional pain. For this reason, it is important to stop and remind yourself: "I need to change this if I am ever to find personal peace with myself. I do not like myself when I act that way, and I really want to change."

It is easy to be a bully in life. It gets you instant effects and immediate results. However, these are not positive results, but they are immediate.

The Defensive Lineman

Teri, a middle-aged secretary, recalled her situation: "It seems like I would be calm for most of the morning. Then, my boss, Mr. Pritchard, would walk in. I could feel my heart pound in my chest. If he asked me to do something, I would clam up, clench my teeth, or say 'I'm not going to get to this right away!' I just hate it when I act like that. I believe I am a kind person, but I also believe he doesn't deserve better treatment."

John, a father of two girls, recounted his actions: "I remember we were standing at the counter ready to buy tickets to enter the museum. There was only one price listed: $10 per person. Our kids were with us, and they were both under two years of age. I knew they wouldn't even remember the trip, and we would carry them the entire time. When the clerk said 'That will be forty dollars,' I started arguing immediately. I was so furious that she would charge full price for those two babies. I ended up slamming my hand on the counter and walking out. I was so irritated! When my friend asked me why I reacted so angrily, I said, 'I can't help it! I'm just assertive!'"

♦ ♦ ♦

Both instances are examples of the Defensive Lineman stance, and in both cases, the individuals reported regrets in how they reacted. It is common for many people to share these reactions. The prevalent thread between them was personal disappointment. Like many other reactions, this disappointment is a sign that you have a conscience. If you experience this painful reaction, it is important to realize that it can serve you well. It may become your motivation to preserve your goodness and reclaim your power.

If you often take a Defensive Lineman approach, it probably means you have trained yourself to think and behave in the following ways:

Your frame of mind: I am always on alert for others when they are not acting exactly the way I want them to. I am always ready to attack. I feel like they are constantly trying to control me, so therefore I will regain control by maintaining firm rebellious behaviors.

What you do to nurture your irrational thinking (your automatic thoughts): When people act this way, I tell myself that these people deserve a good lashing! They have got it coming! I will not let anyone walk all over me! It is such a blessing for me to be in this world; otherwise, no one else would keep these people in their place.

How you get stuck: I sometimes realize that I have developed attitudes toward certain types of people. I just tell myself I seem to have a problem with all bosses…clerks…waitresses… drivers. And I start believing that certain people are rotten and do not deserve good treatment!

How to get unstuck by tapping into your strengths (turning your energy from negative to positive): First, embrace the fact that you are misusing all of your positive energy. Your positive energy is turning into wasted energy because you are not using your strengths to develop others; you are promoting the jerk's behaviors.

Your positive strengths and skill sets:

- You are very sensitive to injustices.
- When action is needed in life, you are the "go-to" person.
- If there is ever an emergency, everyone wants you on their team because you are a doer.

Your misguided behaviors:

- You see it as your job to be judge and jury so you can punish everyone for their behaviors.
- Your need to be right exceeds your need to be civil.
- Deep in your heart, you do not like it when you exercise scrambled hostility. Start using your sensitivity to change others for the good and not to help them maintain their behaviors.

Goals to enhance your skill sets:

- Adopt a goal to drop the hypersensitivity. If you feel you are in a combat situation every day, you will sustain a lot of wounds and scars.
- Take note of how many battles or fights you are involved in throughout the day. Even one battle a day is too many.
- Make it your goal to develop emotional capital—the battles and fights will result only in emotional arthritis. People do not wake up each day with the intent to make your life miserable (but that clerk just loves to control others... my boss tries to get under my skin every day...). You just have trained yourself to see them this way.

> No one can make you feel inferior without your consent.
>
> —*Eleanor Roosevelt*

The Doormat

Kay sat down to take a break. Everyone loved Kay, but over the past year, it was obvious that her health had deteriorated. "I just don't know what to do," she said. "This morning I walked into Mr. Carrigan's office, but before I walked in, I was standing outside the door telling another friend that I would pick her up at lunchtime. Then, when I walked into the office just to get some papers signed, Mr. Carrigan tore the papers out of my hand and shouted, 'Why don't you ever do anything nice for me!' When he yells at me, I freeze, and I don't know what to do! The more I treat him nicely, the meaner he gets."

Kay thrived in her job for years—until the arrival of Mr. Carrigan. She was the sweetest worker the office had ever seen. She was also a Doormat. Under her previous boss, she was appreciated for her selfless spirit, but under Mr. Carrigan's supervision, her life was spiraling downward. Everyone wished they could throw her a life preserver, but they were also busy just trying to avoid Mr. Carrigan's meanness.

The problem for Kay is the mixture of guilt, sadness, and regret that she never seems to be able to step forward to address the poor treatment she receives from her boss. She loves what she does and feels secure knowing where the next check is coming from but can hardly live with herself every time she lets these things happen. Most of the time, she feels as though she has let herself down.

Your frame of mind: All of us have our place in this world, and I realize that my limited potential always will leave me vulnerable. I seem to be unluckier than others because I always seem to get the mean boss, the mean relative, or the mean neighbor. I feel like I am always saying, "I'll always be here. Feel free to clean your feet on me."

What you do to nurture your irrational thinking (your automatic thoughts): I'm on this earth to absorb others' pain. It's my job! I deserve it! You have the right to abuse me; I'm only a low life form; I don't deserve any better treatment. It seems like all of the people in the world with power tend to take advantage of me.

How you get stuck: I'll never, ever, ever, ever have the skills, be as strong as others, be bold enough or strong enough to stand up to these people. I just know that if I do stand up, I will be worse off...lose my job...lose my friends.... I keep thinking if I treat them nicely, then eventually they will treat me nicely. Besides, most of their needs are probably more important than mine.

How to get unstuck by tapping into your strengths (turning your energy from negative to positive): You are a Doormat, and you are unable to access the tools to defend yourself. People with dirty shoes love doormats and always seem to find you, and they scare you to death. This style of relating comes down to two fundamental experiences: the fear of the jerk, and the fear of the unknown if you take a risk.

Your positive strengths and skill sets:

- Doormats are some of the most loving, kind, and generous people on the planet.

- You have a tremendous talent to love others even when they don't seem to deserve it.

Your misguided behaviors:

- You love all others deeply, but you don't believe your life is as valuable as theirs. However, your life and your time are at least as valuable as theirs. Do not let anyone convince you otherwise. If they try to get you to believe their lives are more important than yours, remember: they are JPN (Just Plain Nuts!).

- You waste a lot of energy absorbing other people's miserable communication styles.

- It's not a crime to be a loving person, but it is a very painful life to allow others to clean their feet on you always.

- You fear taking risks because of the erroneous belief that it is impossible to combine firmness with a caring position.

- You hurt inside when you allow yourself to be mistreated but fail to work toward solutions.

Goals to enhance your skill sets:

- Make a goal to continue to please but not be stomped upon. Your struggle will be to practice addressing the process of your communication (more on this later).

- It is not that you need more kindness (you have got plenty of that). What you need are skills to accompany your selflessness.

- Find a time, place, and mutual calm mood to step forward and communicate to the other person how much these behaviors hurt you. Until you do, there will be hundreds of people who will suck the life out of you because you have chosen to own their problems.

Don't bother just to be better than your contemporaries or your predecessors. Try to be better than yourself.

—*William Faulkner*

The Simmering Stew

Dennis left the meeting feeling uneasy. "What did she mean by that comment? Why is she so rude to me? What could I possibly have done to deserve that?"

At 3:00 a.m., Dennis tossed and turned as he tried to sleep. He stared at the ceiling, thinking about being mistreated, and he could not stop thinking about how he felt his colleague had taken advantage of him.

A week later, Dennis was thoroughly exhausted from the lack of sleep and his inability to stop thinking about all of the conflicts in his life.

◆ ◆ ◆

Jack waved his arms frantically as he hustled his family to the exit at the stadium. "Hurry up, hurry up, hurry up!"

His ten-year-old son asked, "Dad, can't we stay until the end of the game?"

"Absolutely not! We have to get moving before all the idiots try to get out of the parking lot at the same time. If we get out now, we will have enough time to have dinner before the evening rush hour gets to the highway. Then, we will be home in time to watch our favorite show."

When no part of the schedule fell into place, Jack spent the day (as usual) lamenting, "We should have left earlier! If we had, my night wouldn't have been ruined."

He would lay awake later that night consumed with how he could have had a better day if only…. Overall, he was consumed with thoughts of regret. "I know I can be pushy. People just don't get it. They tell me I'm pushing others away, but I don't know any other way. They just cannot see my need for an efficient way of life."

◆ ◆ ◆

Jack and Dennis are both choosing to react to life's stressors as a Simmering Stew. They are however, distinctly different-flavored stews. Dennis is a Lamb Stew who experiences a passive and frustrated form of obsession. Jack is a Spicy Beef Stew who obsesses in anger and aggressive obsessions.

Your frame of mind: Something is terribly wrong. This tension never seems to go away. These obsessions are disturbing my lifestyle. They get in the way of moving forward, and sometimes they get in the way of my personal relationships. I know the obsessions are causing me to deteriorate, but I just cannot stop them.

Lamb Stew: I'm constantly hurting because I want to fix this connection. I'm inadequate.

Spicy Beef Stew: I'm constantly hurting because others won't behave the way they should. I'm brilliant because I can see patterns, shortcuts through traffic, short lines in the store, the quickest way out of a parking lot, and the quickest exit from a movie. People are inadequate.

What you do to nurture your irrational thinking (your automatic thoughts): Lamb Stew: I must be doing something. There must be a perfect solution somewhere. But it seems like I will spend my entire lifetime chasing it and never finding it.

Spicy Beef Stew: Snails seem to find their way into my path.... Everywhere I go.... Every time I get there.... These people always.... No one ever... They never.... The lines are long all the time! Other people always mistreat me!

How you get stuck: You not only need to turn down the internal crock pot; you need to turn it off. Most of the time, you are on simmer, and often you are cranked up to full power. You have magnified nearly every incident in life to such an extent that the world could not possibly have the chance to treat you right or live up to your expectations about how life should proceed. Soon the stewing turns into a self-perpetuating string of obsessions in which you notice nothing but the tension.

Lamb Stew: I mean well, but my temperature keeps rising. I can't seem to find a way to turn off the thoughts. They automatically enter my head whether I'm working, sleeping, recreating, or trying to have fun!

Spicy Beef Stew: Mean People! Slow clerks! Traffic! Long lines! Everywhere I go, life feeds me tension. I've set up my daily map to go a certain way: fifteen minutes to get to the store, two minutes in line, five minutes maximum for this shopping trip! Somehow, the rest of the world just has no idea of what it's like to get the most out of a day. It's the same everywhere! I know how to meet a deadline! I know how to plan a vacation! I know how to plan an evening! What are you saying? I'm hard to be around? No, the rest of the world is simply getting dumber by the hour.

How to get unstuck by tapping into your strengths (turning your energy from negative to positive):

Your positive strengths and skill sets:

- You have an extraordinary ability to be efficient.
- You are a great problem-solver.
- You are a great judge of efficiency.

Your misguided behaviors:

- People are people. They are not like you, and you simply are putting too much energy into the parts of life that lack perfect structure.

- In the end, you have a conscience, but in the heat of the moment, you personalize things. For the Lamb Stew, it is a matter of trying to be everything to everybody. For the Spicy Beef Stew, it's as if people are in your way.

- When common sense creeps in, the Lamb Stew has moments when he or she realizes the impossible task of pleasing everyone. The Spicy Beef Stew realizes that he or she is poisoning his or her relationships.

Goals to enhance your skill sets:

- Listen closely to the start of your sentences when you are frustrated. "Everywhere I go.... Every time I get there.... These people always.... No one ever.... They never.... The lines aren't long sometimes; they are long all the time! They always mistreat me!" Notice that the people who are occupied with stewing over the miserable aspects of their life most often use absolutes. The lines are not long sometimes, they are long all the time! Other people are not mistreating them once in a while; they *always* mistreat them! The first step is to eliminate the all-or-nothing thinking.

- As a Beef Stew, you acquired the terrible habit of focusing on the things that are not going right. After a while, you even find it difficult to realize, recognize, or appreciate the moments when life is smooth. You now are wasting good moments by obsessing on the thing that did not go right five minutes ago! Stop and breathe, and stay in the moment.

- Realize that deadlines and resolutions only need to be applied to certain things—not everything.

- You cannot please everyone, and you cannot take care of 100 demands every day. This carries over into the simplest things: family outings, shopping, and dining. You become hard to be around, and you lose ground in the relationships closest to you.

- Your goal should be to acquire more sensitivity to different people's styles and different paces. Your loved ones will begin to resent you if you keep pushing your pace and obsessive way of thinking.

- Other people do not constantly jeopardize your efficiency. You just see it that way. Realize that life is fair, and it is not inherently set up to make you crazy.

- Find your flow (see skills in Step Six) because until you do, you will make your life and your loved ones' lives a self-constructed living hell. Every moment you spend obsessing on things you cannot control is a moment in which it is impossible to be a good friend, co-worker, spouse, or parent.

> Nothing can bring you peace but yourself.
> —Ralph Waldo Emerson

The Commiserator

Greg complained to his co-workers, "This used to be such a great place to work!" Every day at lunchtime he would become energized when he found others who would agree and pick apart the current status of the workplace. If others were not as miserable as he was, they were, in his mind, oblivious to the real problems of the world.

"It seemed like she was loyal, but then, in the blink of an eye, she turned on me. I just can't forgive her," said Danielle. After a period of time on her job, she became increasingly isolated, less trusting, and more suspicious of those who tried to show her care. Danielle had at least one friend, Jim, in whom she confided (and he agreed) that others tend to be shallow. When others disagreed with her, she immediately viewed them as disloyal.

♦ ♦ ♦

Commiserators get their name from the word stems *miserable* and *co*. The *co* prefix indicates a tendency to be codependent (let's do it together!), but the goal is to find others who will join them in misery. They find others who agree with them because it is the only security they have, but they ride a roller coaster through life. If you agree with me, you are a good person. If you do not agree, you are back stabbing and abandoning me. Commiserators have a lifetime of back-to-back honeymoons with jobs, locations, relationships, and every new person they meet. They are excited to meet new people, get new jobs, and have new experiences. Then, they are disappointed when flaws begin to surface. Commiserators keep life on extremes: "Best job I ever had. Six months later, she turned on me. This place went downhill." In their heart, Commiserators feel the pain. "I hang out with and seek out people I don't want to be like, but at least it explains why I'm miserable. They understand me."

Your frame of mind: I just can't understand why I place all my faith in the world, and it ends up turning out bad. It doesn't just have its bumps; I hit sinkholes that seem to jar me for the rest of my life. It's just not worth investing in anymore. I'm such a loving and trusting person, but I lost faith in so many people after they turned their backs on me.

What you do to nurture your irrational thinking (your automatic thoughts): I've had a lifetime of abandonment. Everybody sees me as a weak person, but I'm certain it's not me. I have some very loyal people who agree. People's true colors seem to come out if I am around them long enough. I place faith in people, and then they crush me. Most others would be miserable too if they only knew what I know.

How you get stuck: You try to find others who agree that this is a rotten world. As long as you can find others who experience this misery, you will not feel so alone in your mistreatment.

How to get unstuck by tapping into your strengths (turning your energy from negative to positive): Anywhere you can find a friend who is hurting, it becomes your place to hang out. Stop saying, "Do you know what the problem is here?"

Stop having honeymoons. People are people. They do not just suddenly go bad every place you live and every place you work.

Your positive strengths and skill sets:

- You are a tremendous gatherer of information.
- You value camaraderie.
- You are able to make connections and find reasons for the way things operate in the world.
- You have great skills in communication and in structuring a message to others, perhaps observing and seeing things that many people may overlook.
- Of all the common reactions, yours has great potential for leadership because you value camaraderie in work and in life.

Your misguided behaviors:

- Your energy goes into substantiating cause and effect, but it never arrives at a more positive solution. Simply put: if you did not get your energy from the problems in life, you would have no energy in life.
- Instead of using your abilities to solve a problem, they go into a rationale for why you feel so bad.
- You value camaraderie, which means you have some innate leadership qualities, but you need to stop seeing human differences as disloyalties. Stop rallying for a battle against the disagreeable, and start rallying for solutions. Disagreements are not the same as disloyalties.
- Instead of leading people toward the promised land, your shtick may be seen as the perpetual "doom and gloomer." You may start to be seen as a negative force. As a Commiserator, others may start to keep things from you because they feel like they have to walk on eggshells when they are around you. The reason people will not share their ideas with you is because your habit is constantly

to cite a "doom and gloom" scenario from the past to tell them that the idea will not work.

Goals to enhance your skill sets:

- As a crusader for justice, you can enhance the status of those around you by gathering data that leads to solutions.

- Stop looking for problems and stop obsessing on how others see the world differently from you. It disallows you to see the path to healing. When you seek out and find your miserable comrades in arms, you lose your ability to make bigger changes in the big picture. Stop seeking only the pessimists who agree with you; start looking for the optimists who are trying new things. Try to make it a habit to listen to the optimists instead of putting on the earmuffs every time they speak.

- As a Commiserator, you never extend an olive branch (an offering of peace). Get rid of the ego, try to mend fences, and nurture relationships in spite of differences. You will be astounded by how good it will make you feel.

- Make it a goal (as hard as it can be) to realize that life is a good thing, and recognize that most people are good-willed. While this sounds simple, you know that the knot in your gut comes from that small part of you that knows it is your fault. Misery loves company, and it is easy to find that company. However, deep inside you know it only makes you angrier when you commiserate your unmet needs. There is a part of you that aches to see the better side of life, but commiserating with others has become your cesspool.

- Realize that life is too short to spend time dwelling on resentments.

> Success comes to those who ignore their setbacks and simply refuse to give up.
>
> —*Laurence G. Bolt*

The Defeated

"There is just nothing else I can do," said Bill. "The more I try, the more it becomes just one more lesson in futility. There's only so much one man can do, and I've tried it all."

Bill was a part of the senior staff but had checked out a long time ago. He had just experienced a confrontation with a co-worker. He had been snapped at repeatedly. "What good is it to throw in my two cents? It's a waste of my time." Whenever anyone disagreed with him, it felt as though he had been choked.

Dara had seen it all: the good, the bad, and the useless effort to change it all. "Twelve years, two months, and three days until retirement. That's where all my energy is going these days; it certainly doesn't do any good to put energy into this place. It's just not worth it anymore. I'll never find the good life with this job."

Dara and Bill share the empty feeling of wondering what happened to those days when we always saw the good in this place, the good in others, the good in tomorrow. Dara and Bill react to jerks much like the Doormat because they feel trampled upon. Unlike the doormat, however, they only can lament the loss of the past. They feel like they have lost a wrestling match, and they have had all the life strangled out of them. People do not necessarily clean their feet on the Defeated (like they do on the Doormat), but the Defeated believe they are in a submission hold. The Doormat does not know what to do; those who are Defeated know what they could do but have lost their will to try to work with others when treated with negativity and rudeness.

Your frame of mind: I'm paralyzed. I long to get back to the good old days, but I can't go back. I was only naïve back then. Now that I see the big picture, I can also see that it's not worth the fight. Look at these scars on my neck! I was choked a long time ago, and I'm not going through that again. If I've learned to mistrust, to stop letting people into my heart, it's because I've had one too many heartbreaks.

What you do to nurture your irrational thinking (your automatic thoughts): You just don't know what it's like to be me. There's nothing anyone can do about it. I gave up a long time ago, but I have my reasons. Somebody give me one good reason why I should care. I know that if I take that chance, my heart will just get stomped on all over again.

How you get stuck: I'm past the tipping point. There's no turning back. Victory will never be in sight. I have a lot of evidence to show you that things will never get better. There are just too many jerks for me ever to have enough energy to deal with all of them. Look at my office; it will never be neat again; who cares anyway! Look at my body; another diet tried and failed. Look at my job; what else would I do? I'm the poster child for stuckness. Besides, what good does it do to think for the future? Look at Fred. He took care of himself then just keeled over one day.

How to get unstuck by tapping into your strengths (turning your energy from negative to positive):

Your positive strengths and skill sets:

- You realize what the good life could look like, and it gnaws away at you. At least you have a glimmer of hope.

- You are sensitive to failure.

- Since you are so sensitive to failure, you have great potential to be a mentor to others who have failed.

- You see others in pain and haven't forgotten what it's like to try and try again. You have the ability to try again; you simply lack the will to execute another move.

- You are a sponge that soaks up the world. You realize that you are in the middle of life and full of life. Your source of internal pain comes from knowing you could try something different but do not.

Your misguided behaviors:

- Instead of saying, "Oh well, there's always another day," you say, "Oh gad, there's another day, but it will probably be just like the last."

- Your rationale for not moving forward is based on your observations of successes and failures. The only ones you count up are the failures, and you use them as a reference.

Goals to enhance your skill sets:

- See each failed event not as a brick in the wall in front of you, but as a stepping stone. Start using experiences as lessons rather than evidence for prosecuting life.

- Allow yourself to journal and take note of the small things that allow you to have success.

- Right now, the only thing that is killing you is not an earthquake or a hurricane or some other major life event, but rather termites. Pick them off one at a time. The little things are killing you.

- Since you are a sponge, absorb more of the sunshine than the rain.

- With all your awareness, you have tremendous insight. Use it to lift others rather than burdening yourself.

> Consistency is contrary to nature, contrary to life.
> The only completely consistent people are the dead.
> —*Aldous Huxley*

The Deer in the Headlights

"I was so embarrassed—I couldn't believe how I was attacked." Kristy just left the meeting and now sat stunned in her office. "What the heck is wrong with me? He attacked me in the meeting, cut me off, and there I was! Stunned! With tears in my eyes! Gosh, it makes me such a nervous wreck! I will never be able to speak up after that!"

Ed shook his head. "I feel so inadequate around those people. When they come after me, I never seem to have that comeback, that retort, that ability to fire back at them. The problem is, I don't want to attack back when I'm attacked. I just wish I had the ability to handle them better."

Kristy and Ed display one of the most common reactions to jerks. They are hurt, choose not to hurt others back, and then feel guilty about how inadequate they felt in that situation. They are stunned at the meanness of others but don't have a mean bone in their bodies; therefore, they often feel they are unequipped to deal with such a hostile world. They are in an emotional state of shock when they are confronted by aggression. It doesn't matter whether they are in line shopping, in a meeting, in a car, or visiting with relatives.

People who demonstrate the Deer in the Headlights reaction may have more potential than any other group. The reason? Above all, they still have faith in people. The classic Deer in the Headlights may be some of the kindest people among us.

They never seem to be prepared for anger and hostility—because they have such great trust in humanity.

Your frame of mind: I'm always off guard. There must be something I'm missing, some skill I never learned; I'm never ready to battle. I should be smarter than this! These things have happened before, and there I go letting it happen again. I must have a target on my back.

What you do to nurture your irrational thinking (your automatic thoughts): Why do I keep setting myself up to get hurt? I'm never going to have the chutzpah, backbone, fortitude, or bravery to be as effective as I would like to be in my job, in my relationships, or in other areas of life.

How you get stuck: You keep questioning yourself in spite of your good intentions. The Deer in the Headlights is an innocent person who believes that others have good will. The problem is that they turn the hurt on themselves, and they tell themselves, "I am being mistreated—I must have done something wrong. I'm always setting myself up for these things. There I was off guard again! How could I let myself do that again!"

How to get unstuck by tapping into your strengths (turning your energy from negative to positive):

Your positive strengths and skill sets:

- You assume that people are good. Give yourself permission to be okay with that.
- You believe that others have the capacity for good.
- You choose to be around positive people because you have an optimistic outlook on life.
- You have faith that others are guided by goodness, and this belief guides your passions. This may make you vulnerable, but you choose to be this way because you do not want to become like the miserable ones.

- You may be exercising the most compassionate of all reactions toward others because you believe humanity is still good at its core.

Your misguided behaviors:

- You beat yourself up when you are stuck.

- You turn painful confrontations into "What am I doing wrong?"

- You cannot stop wondering if you could have done something different when you get stunned by others' cruelty.

- You have sleepless nights because you keep the loop playing over: "What did I do wrong in that situation? Why does it always seem like I'm so vulnerable in these situations?"

Goals to enhance your skill sets:

- Keep the tension in its compartment. If the tension consumed five minutes at the meeting, leave the tension there. Sometimes, being around tense people is much like being at the dentist; keep the faith that it will be over soon.

- Keep the goodness in your heart. Always let yourself be open and vulnerable. Embrace your vulnerability as a strength and an asset, not a liability.

- Stick with others who believe that life is still good. Realize that the jerks are more stuck than you! Never lose your sweetness.

- When you feel stunned after a confrontation, realize that it is your faith in people, your assumption that humans are good, that makes you feel vulnerable. At your heart, you are a counselor of good will. Use that skill to help others through problems like these.

- If negative energy can band together, so can positive energy. Keep up the effort; your conscience wouldn't allow you to do anything else.

> When I die, I'm going to leave my body to science fiction.
>
> *—Steven Wright*

The long-term effect of jerks

First and Foremost: Death
Your mind will decide to allow the jerks to kill you.

If you are aware of your reactions to jerks, the good news is this: you are alive and still concerned, and you have not given up hope. The bad news is this, however: if you keep reacting to jerks the way you have (in unproductive and destructive ways), you will die sooner than you would like.

Most of our reactions to jerks have one thing in common: they are contrary to the nature of human survival. Psychologists and biologists have known for years that distress changes our physical makeup. With more stress, we have more accidents due to poor concentration. We have more illnesses due to the breakdown of our immunity systems. Our lives lose balance because we have worse health habits when we are distressed, and sadly, distressed people have more family problems and divorces because the pain is felt most by those in our closest relationships. Simply stated: our relationships take a beating.

In the extreme, we also know that those who confront the wrong jerk at the wrong time end up on the wrong end of a car accident, or the wrong end of someone's revenge, or the wrong end of a weapon. For these reasons, it is important to take action to deal with the jerks as soon as we can. If we do not, our lives fall apart. Another thing that happens when we fail to deal effectively with jerks is that we adopt new habits to replace the comfort we lost. We eat more, sleep less, take more medications, exercise less, avoid healthy outlets, poison our own relationships, and lose sight of the bigger picture. It is all because we are overwhelmed with the pain in this world and fail to use our natural instincts to deal with it.

> If you haven't any charity in your heart,
> you have the worst kind of heart trouble.
>
> —*Bob Hope*

Ineffective living

One of the saddest tragedies is the loss of human potential. When we get caught up in the world of jerks, it keeps us from being a good friend, co-worker, Mom, Dad, lover, or companion. For every minute we spend in the agonizing world of the jerk, we have lost a minute of life that we cannot retrieve. We are jeopardizing the good, charitable, and generous part of our personality.

It is wise to be aware of the pain. However, our problems begin when we absorb the pain. When we absorb pain, we also lose meaning in life. We start to tell ourselves that good, meaningful, and purposeful lives are for the lucky, the affluent, or the famous.

When we realize all the waste that takes place by getting caught up in the world of jerks, we remind ourselves that giving is still good. Generosity of the spirit is the best generosity we will ever know, and just because someone slams a door in our face, we should not shut others out.

Sometimes jerks not only will justify their behavior, but they also believe that they have some profound insight that no one else does. They also may believe that their situation is unique, and therefore they are entitled to be a jerk. "When I have to talk to this person for forty minutes and they just don't get it, I think I have the right to tell them like it is. If you had to be around this person as long as I have, you would blow up too."

The worst hypocrisy is when people twist a philosophy or religion to justify meanness. I recently witnessed a conversation in which a person was on a tirade about how he was going to get even. The other person tried to soften the conversation by suggesting a religious perspective: "Yes, but doesn't the Lord also want us to forgive?" The response from the tirading aggressive person was, "Forgiveness is fine, but the Lord also insists on justice; the Lord also said 'Vengeance is mine!'"

The hostile individual spends a lot of mental energy to justify cruelty. In his or her mind, cruelty has its place, and you cannot argue with God because God is always right!

Throughout human history, religion and philosophy have been wonderful sources of wisdom and guidance. As we delve into the wisdom of the Hindu, Muslim, Christian, Jew, American Indian, we have to keep in mind that there are a lot of wonderful, compassionate sentiments that are derived from philosophical and religious teachings. Many of these philosophical foundations speak of a spiritual dimension that we can carry with us in all that we do. The greater questions for the spiritually driven individual are: "What is my essence?" and "Do I carry this in all that I think and do?" You cannot say, "I'm a deeply religious and devout follower of my religion" while constantly creating irrational, anger-filled scenarios in your head. You cannot call yourself a follower of God, Jesus, Buddha, or Allah whilst being consumed with the destruction of your fellow human beings. Again, we need to turn inward to ask: "Am I living the spiritual essence that I espouse to others?" Every religion can be used either for promoting peace or for fanatical condemnation. In either case, your thoughts are your spiritual essence. Buddha once said, "To know and to not do is not really to know." If our constant companion is an aggressive thought, we need to revisit our spiritual essence. When we are consumed with thoughts of ill will, we truly do not know.

When we twist a religion or philosophy to suit our aggressive needs, we have committed an injustice to that religion. We also have created a life of ineffective living because we have not used common sense or wisdom to solve our problem. Wisdom is distinctly separate from intelligence. We know people who are severely cognitively impaired, yet they are wise when it comes to peaceful relationships. We also know of people who have high IQs, yet they are horrible jerks.

You can have an IQ of 60 or 160, and it may not determine whether you are able to get along with others. You can watch two intellectually disabled children try to solve a conflict. Some will practice gentleness, and others will physically strike out. You can sit in a meeting with relatively intelligent people, and the same will hold true; some will hit back when challenged (perhaps through sneakiness, meanness, or cruel comments), and others will not. This is evidence that all humans have the capability of striking back at others, but likewise it is also evidence that all human beings have the capability for peaceful interactions. The need to strike back may be reactive or just a personal habit born of the belief that the whole world is a constant source of persecution. Again, our spiritual essence is the collection of thoughts we carry with us into these situations.

We need to embrace the idea that there is a separate form of intelligence distinctively independent from what we know to be traditional "intelligence." This aptitude is an "intellect of the compassionate spirit and the kind heart," and its goal is not to solve just an individual's problems, but the problems of humanity. This kind of intelligence also determines one's personal feelings of integrity for a life well lived. We should never give up hope that anyone could acquire this type of intelligence; even Scrooge eventually learned despite his misguided need for domination of others. He even learned to laugh at himself!

We can certainly recognize that defensive reactions may be natural. Perhaps we could even recognize some aspects of self-preservation. However, we also see people who can rise above cruelty and prove that humans are capable of peaceful coexistence. In doing so, we will have moved to an entirely different plane of existence in which wisdom for compatibility serves a greater long-term self-preservation, in addition to enhancing the preservation of the species. Briefly: everyone lives longer when we stop acting like jerks.

> Many do not know that we are here in this world to live in harmony.
>
> —Buddha

Insanity

I once had a client in therapy named George. He was 52 years old and stood around 5'3" tall. George was a soft-spoken, big-hearted, gentle little man with a dimpled smile and a full head of grey hair. He was experiencing anxiety and depression, and as he cried in my office, he shared a story that had never left him: "When I was six years old, I was being raised by my aunt and uncle. My aunt would fall asleep early every evening because she was drunk. I was afraid most nights when my uncle would come home after a night of drinking, as usually he was drunk and violent. There was a safe place I had in the corner under a great big heavy iron bed. Whenever I heard him coming, I would scramble around and find my kitten, which was the only thing in the world that mattered to me. Then I would crawl under the bed and hold my kitty until he left. This one night I heard him come through the door, and I ran around but couldn't find my kitty. I had to dive under the bed by myself. As usual, he was angry and yelled at me from above the bed. But this time was different. He screamed, 'You want to hide from me?! You want to hide from me? Well, hide with this!' He grabbed my kitty, broke its neck, then threw it under the bed where it landed on my chest, dead."

George sobbed as he told the story, and I could not help myself but to cry with him. I also knew that I would never judge him for all the anxiety, fear, or depression he would experience in his life. I remember for many nights that followed, I would be awake at 3:00 in the morning and wonder, "How can any human being do that to another? How could anyone do that to a six-year-old?"

I clearly remember that dimpled smile and the gentle spirit that George brought to everyone he met, and if anyone had the right to be bitter, angry, or resentful toward life, it was George. But he chose not to. He was a gentle father, a devoted spouse, but a broken, tortured man. In spite of his pain, he chose goodness over ill will and bitterness.

The worst kind of insanity is not when a person gets panic attacks or is sad because he or she is lonely. The worst kind of insanity is not in the form of schizophrenia when one hears voices and experiences hallucinations. It is not in the moments when we are clinically depressed due to our losses, nor is it when we have traumatic distress because of our past. These are often normal reactions to abnormal situations, or they may be conditions we cannot change. The worst kind of insanity is when we choose to be insane. When we knowingly inflict pain on another human being—this is the worst kind of insanity. When we choose to humiliate a co-worker because our personal needs are not being met, we have lost our sanity. When we snap irretrievable words at our loved ones because we are having a crabby, crampy, tired day, we have lost our sanity. When we disparage someone with the intent to portray ourselves as superior to them, we have lost our sanity. When we choose to give a child pain because we are upset, we have lost our sanity.

These acts of insanity may not be to the pathological degree to which George had to suffer. It may only be a small moment when we steal a child's self-worth or rob a clerk of her dignity, but nonetheless, it is still the worst kind of insanity because we are choosing to inflict madness on others.

We also may hear someone say, "I just can't help myself!" I wonder how you would act if I offered you twenty million dollars if you could go for a month without berating others, yelling at your children, disparaging someone behind his back, or snapping at your loved ones. Would you change? Yes, you would give it more effort than any other endeavor you have ever had. Why? Because it would become a top priority in your life. Is your wife, spouse, child, co-worker, neighbor, or relative worth twenty million dollars? I hear people say, "My family is the most important thing in my life!" But sadly, they treat a stray cat better than their loved ones. They are fooling themselves. Apparently, the person who says, "I just can't help myself," places little value on others. It is not that you cannot help yourself; it is a matter of not helping yourself.

There is enough pain in the world just the way it is. Hurricanes, storms, earthquakes, famine, flooding, cancer, and AIDS provide enough pain for humanity. Would it not make better sense to put our energies into relieving pain? If we go through a single day and pursue pain for others, obsess on pain for others, or inflict pain on others, we have lost our ability in those moments to make the world a better place, and this is the worst kind of insanity.

George does not have a choice about whether nightmares will enter his sleep tonight, but we have the choice to be patient, or kind, or gentle. We can exercise goodness even in life's most difficult times.

Step Three:

Understand Your Personal Obstacles

The ten most paralyzing mental myths when dealing with jerks

> The growth of wisdom may be gauged accurately by the decline of ill-temper.
>
> —*Friedrick Nietzche*

When we create irrational ideas to support our cruelty toward others, we have become delusional and irrational. They are mental myths, but they are also a form of convenient misery, and their purpose is to move the blame from ourselves to those forces around us that we believe we cannot control.

The following paralyzing comments are very common. The more we are acting like a jerk, the more often we may say them. If these comments are coming from the person in the mirror, it is time to get to work. If we hear ourselves saying these things, or if we find ourselves thinking these things, our habits of thinking have become our myths. They are excuses that may cause our lives to spiral downward into self-persecution, paranoia, and pain. And they may cause us to become more cruel to others.

> Rudeness is the weak man's imitation of strength.
> —Eric Hoffer

1. I tell it like it is, and people just can't handle the truth!

This myth may expose our need to be two things: an expert in everything, and always right about everything. This myth is used to justify excessive emotions and a raised voice in communicating with others. Raised voices rarely have anything to do with the issue; they have more to do with a battle for power. The self-induced myth that people just cannot handle the truth is a delusion that makes us incapable of seeing that there are many truths in this world. We may have a legitimate argument, but the stronger the argument, the greater the need for diplomacy in every discussion we have. In a calm person's heart, he or she realizes that there is no need to become over-emotional every time someone does not see things the same way. In a restless person's heart, the scream: "People just can't handle the truth!" is merely an expression of frustration. It is not that they cannot handle the truth; they cannot handle our aggressive approach.

This myth is also a very powerful and negative influence on the way we treat people in a lot of everyday situations. I once worked with a person who believed she was a strong, assertive personality. She held the belief that day-to-day cruelty is justifiable. She was having a conflict with a secretary and was disrespectful toward her. Afterwards, I suggested that she could get a lot farther with a little kindness. Her response was, "I don't suck up to anyone!" This response is common and shows two things. First, it indicates that this person condones rude behavior and that the other person not only deserved this meanness, but that he or she was also at fault for not acting according to her expectations. Second, she sees kindness as a weakness. Most certainly, she believes that "If I attempt to iron things out, if I try to collaborate, if I extend good will in the face of tension, then I am weak!"

When we cling to this myth, we stubbornly keep ourselves from the ability to nurture relationships or find common ground. As long as we believe that others just cannot handle the truth, and we are the only ones who can tell it like it is, we will make our lives lonelier and more pathetic.

The myth can also result in misconceptions about pride. In our culture, we often distort the notion or idea of pride. We may think, "I won't bend; I'm just too proud!" However, to those around you, it is clear: they do not see you as a proud person but as stubborn. If we are truly proud, we exercise our best behavior, not our worst or most destructive (and then hide behind the word proud as though it were a badge of character). It would be like saying you are proud of your home, then go bashing in all the windows. When we are proud of something, we display it in its best light, not its worst.

When we distort the notion of pride to support our aggression, we actually have revealed our weakness and our inability to validate others' lives as being as important as our own. It is not the case that people cannot handle the truth; they cannot handle a jerk. Power comes in the selection of words, not in their volume or caustic nature.

> If life was fair, Elvis would be alive and all the
> impersonators would be dead.
>
> —*Johnny Carson*

2. I'm right! Therefore, I'm righteous!

This myth evolves as a remnant of adolescent thinking. If you listen to adolescents, they will repeat this saying over and over: "It's not fair! It's not fair! It's not fair!" When we are adolescents and striving to form our identity, we become consumed with obtaining the right to be treated as an adult. This is a natural part of adolescence, but not a natural part of a well-balanced adult. We understand that our views of fairness need to be merged with the idea that we cannot have everything.

In our adult life, it is important that we stand up against unfairness, especially when it comes to civil rights. However, when we put our energies into playing judge and jury for all areas of unfairness, we will be fighting a lot of empty battles. We will be fighting ghosts our whole life.

Do you really think that slowing down in the fast lane on the highway will change the world and make other people better drivers? Do you really think you are "teaching someone a good lesson" when you run your car up on their bumper at 65 miles per hour because "they shouldn't be driving so slow in the fast lane—THAT WILL TEACH THEM!"

We may find ourselves saying, "But they deserve it!" It is not our personal job to achieve this form of justice, and when we do, we are not making the world a safer place, but rather we are making it a more dangerous place. And each time we do this, we are placing our one and only life in a dangerous situation.

> For peace of mind, resign as general manager of the universe.
>
> *—Larry Eisenberg*

Do you really believe it is your job to teach everybody a lesson by being mean to them? "But that waitress had it coming!"

Life is not fair, but we Americans live in a country that was designed to promote fairness. The system was constructed by people who believed in checks and balances, decency, civility, and freedom. When we exercise road rage, shopping rage, or bullying, we are practicing tyranny, not democracy. The "not fair" excuse provides us with a belief that we have the right to impose our own version of fairness, even if it means steamrolling others, running people off the road, or using propaganda to win our battle.

This myth results in a need to deliver our interpretation of justice in all situations. Justice is best left to a democratic voice and the majority of people. If we are running around believing that we have the right to road rage, point out others' mistakes, and put others in their place, we are making the world a more difficult place to live, rather than a better one. It also espouses the belief that we think we know more than the rest of society. In other words, who should stop people from speeding at unsafe speeds? What good would it do if we announced, "From now on, we won't have any state patrol officers on the highway because we are going to leave it up to everyone else out there to take the law into their own hands and teach these people a lesson if you see them speeding."

We need to report violations of our laws but not take the laws into our own hands. If everyone became judge and jury, we would have social anarchy. It is one thing to defend ourselves; it is entirely something different when we lash out.

When we believe that lashing out is justified, we are placing everyone in danger. When we are truly acting on the side of justice, we use diplomacy and a civilized system to alter the course of the world.

If we look at human history, we can see incredible examples of people acting on the side of justice. There are many cases in history in which horrible injustices have occurred, but it was the united masses who made changes, not vigilantes. In India, the masses who objected to the injustices of British Rule, not a desperate extremist, had the most effect. It was a gentle, soft-spoken man named Gandhi who asserted his message without raising a fist.

When the peaceful protests of the '60s resulted in the dismantling of the unjust segregation policies, it was the will of the majority who changed the way we think, not the renegade with a machine gun who wanted single-handedly to punish the world. It was done with conviction, principles, and nonviolence. There are certainly times when brute force needs to be exercised to stop the danger of an attack, but ask yourself "Is my life in danger because I allowed you into my lane on the highway? Is it really life and death?" Brute force may stop a behavior, but it does not teach a new one.

The best way to battle injustices is to use common sense and the will of the people, not irrationality and the will of one. We also can look at a microcosm of society and see where people prosper. Families, businesses, and communities thrive best when they have rules of order decided by the group. If it is an iron fist ruling from the top down, we know that members of that group resent the oppression. In our own lives, we know people who were ruled by authoritarian parents, bosses, and dictatorships. The end result was a disturbed or broken individual who became obsessed with either escaping the system or destroying it.

Irrational, rude tirades often are followed by irrational claims of, "But I am right!" Believing that we are right about something does not authorize us to indulge in idiotic behavior. This excuse allows us to justify excessive emotions and raised voices in communicating with others. Verbal abuse rarely has anything to do with the issue; it has more to do with a battle for power. When we exercise rudeness, most of the time it means we have run out of the proper words to conclude our argument. We can no longer muster the appropriate words to give others a compelling reason to reconsider their position, and we resort to bullying. So it is like saying, "If you, the idiot, are not 'getting it' (agreeing with me), I (with the infallible viewpoint) have every right to abuse you verbally, to tell you to 'shut up,' and even to throw personal slanders in your direction."

Children, on one hand, learn respectful civil debate in their classrooms, then tune into major propaganda television programs and learn that verbal bullying is acceptable, abuse is commendable, and rudeness is admirable. These programs are an insult to human decency.

> You can't have everything. Where would you put it?
>
> —*Steven Wright*

3. There are "my rules" for life that must be followed!

Think about the last time you or someone else exclaimed, "I'm having a horrible day!" More accurately, we should say, "I'm miserable today because things aren't happening according to my rules!"

The problem is that if I create "Steve's rules," I have made up my mind that a day is good only if everything goes my way. This is an exercise in egotism because I believe that I have the right to live in a hectic world with no hitches or consequences attached to my serene existence.

In other words, we want a world of cell phones, cars, computers, and plasma TVs, but how dare you upset my serenity! We want to live in the midst of a social system with all the societal perks but without any of the inconveniences. If this is the case, we need a wake-up call to remind us of the plain truth: there always will be inconsistencies in life, and if these upset us, then we need to adapt to them.

When we believe the world is controlling us, we end up resenting anyone or any circumstance that violates "Steve's rules," or "Jane's rules," or "Bill's rules." It's like saying, "The day is good only if everyone acts according to my sense of right or wrong! I'm having a terrible day due to my terrible fight with traffic, terrible kids, terrible husband, terrible boss, and that terrible Mother Nature who made it rain today! How was my day? Miserable! These people had the audacity to refuse to live up to Steve's rules! Meetings should never run late! There must never be long lines! There must never be a raise in rates for my electric bill! There must never be a breakdown in my car! All the traffic in my lane must be smooth! Heaven forbid that I should ever have to reset my cruise control! No one should ask me (the Prince of Steve's world) to do extra work today! There must be no crumbs on the floor, dishes in the sink, or barking dogs! These things violate Steve's rules! How dare anyone violate Steve's rules?"

Every one of us has to admit that we may be guilty of this myth. We create really stupid rules for what we believe is a good or bad day. Famed psychologist Albert Ellis referred to this as "musterbation." Ellis also said that too many "shoulds" result in us "shoulding all over ourselves."

Sometimes we even go as far as demonizing those people and things that we think control our happiness. One of the most profound sentiments ever conveyed by Gandhi was in response to the ongoing religious wars in India. In the midst of the turmoil, people were blaming and demonizing those who they believed were the cause of their pain. Gandhi said, "The only devils in the world are those running around in our own hearts, and that is where all our battles ought to be fought."

If you are battling traffic, long lines, and people who have a different style of living than you, then you are most certainly fighting on the wrong battlefield. Fight the battle in your heart, and there will be no battlefields in your day.

> I have never been disabled in my dreams.
> —*Christopher Reeves*

4. There's nothing I can do about it!

Many among us cannot imagine what it would be like to find strength for a real crisis because so many of us have never endured real crises. Losing a loved one in a terrorist attack, being the victim of a meaningless random crime, enduring a bizarre medical affliction, or losing a loved one to an act of nature are all real crises. These are things you cannot change, and they are real tragedies. They also require more strength than many of us can imagine.

There are a lot of people who go about their daily routines with assorted "imaginary crises" such as, "I can't find a parking spot!" or "We're out of coffee!" Sometimes it is hard to imagine how their world would be rocked if they had a real crisis.

When Christopher Reeves suffered a permanent disability after being thrown from a horse, he went from a situation in which he was on top of the world as a Hollywood actor (known for his Superman movies) to one of near helplessness in a matter of moments. He went from being physically active to a quadriplegic in one second. The lesson he taught us was that we cannot always change our circumstances and our fate, but we can change our thoughts about them. He lost his physical potential but refused to give up his emotional, psychological, and spiritual potential. Many believe that his greatest contributions to humanity came after the accident as he inspired others, raised millions of dollars for research, and became an activist for the rights of those with disabilities. He lost his body, but he never lost hope.

When we believe that "there's nothing I can do about my neighbor... my boss... my kids... my job...," we need to re-evaluate our lives. Not only can we do something with a new behavior; we also can change the way we think about it. If we buy into the myth "There's nothing I can do about it," we have made a conscious decision to allow people and things to control our thoughts. In fact, we have given up on the one thing which we can create in abundance (and it costs us nothing). This wonderful thing is hope.

In order for hope to be real, it cannot be a cliché; it has to be a manner of living every day. We often confuse hope with wishing. If we are hoping that humanity will stop being cruel but are not doing something about it, we are simply being wishful. Often we think we are hopeful, but if the hope is not accompanied by action, all we are doing is waiting and complaining. The civil rights movement was never founded on wishes; it was a deliberate commitment to care. It was a collective movement of purposeful behaviors, and those committed individuals were not waiting for someone else to step up to the plate. Wishful people hesitate and may claim that "the time is not right," but for them, the time will never be right because the courage to act is never summoned.

When people give up hope, they become apathetic and cynical. When we are cynical, we see the doom and gloom in others' views, and we are quick to point out that the optimist is an idiot. Recently I was working with a group of people who were trying to resolve a conflict with another person. One person kept insisting that everyone go behind this person's back. Several people believed that the decent thing to do was to be forthright. The cynic told everyone, "Oh, you just watch! You'll go and be nice, extend the olive branch, and as soon as you turn around, they will take that olive branch and stick it where the sun doesn't shine! You just wait. You'll see I'm right!"

The group took the high road, extended the olive branch, and...they were rejected. The cynic was in all his glory: "I told you it wouldn't work! I know these people!"

A very kind and pleasant woman in our group responded with, "Being realistic, I didn't have a real high expectation, but I did hold out hope, and I still hope that this person will one day turn the corner. You never know, if enough people keep trying to be nice, she may one day find peace, and even if we only had a remote chance of getting through, it was worth it to me to try. I want to keep trying because I fear that if I don't, I may become as miserable as they are. I know we did the right thing, and that's enough for me."

In the end, the group became much closer. Collectively, they had more resolve and more respect for themselves and for one another. In the end, it was worth it. In the end, hope and decency won out. It always does.

> Egotism is the anesthetic that dulls the pain of stupidity.
>
> —*Frank Leahy*

5. I can't help it! I'm passionate!

Many of us are guilty of using "passion" as a license for ill-tempered behavior. Passion is no excuse for crazy. All of us have witnessed a person in the act of throwing a tantrum. We all have experienced the moment when we try to calm him down and he responds with, "I can't help it! I'm passionate."

In these moments, are we suggesting that everyone else is not as passionate as we are? I am very passionate about my baseball team, but that does not give me the right to run on the field and yell at the umpire if I disagree. I am very passionate about politics, but that does not give me the right to harm others, make disparaging remarks about their character, or encourage hate simply because I oppose their views. Most of us are passionate about a lot of things, but we do not have the right to violate others to voice our views. We should never confuse passion with egotism. Our ego has led us to believe that our passion is our license for crazy.

When we are angry and miserable, we often will hide behind statements like, "I'm just assertive…. I'm a passionate person…. I'm intensely devoted to this, and that is why I go after people!"

It does not matter whether you are a teacher or a student, a parent or a child, a boss or an entry-level worker, an administrator or a staff member; it is entirely possible to be very firm and very caring at the same time. We can make any point without attacking, screaming, rudeness, or hostility.

When we subscribe to the "I'm passionate" philosophy, we believe in the misperception that the most assertive people are those who are the quickest, loudest, most verbal, and most forceful. True assertiveness is a skill that opens doors to a two-way street. It is based on this premise: I will not allow you to violate me or violate the rights of others, and in communicating this to you, I will not, under any circumstances, violate you in speech or behavior either. Assertiveness is a personal ground rule for how I will communicate with you.

We can be kind and firm at the same time. We can be persistent and respectful at the same time. We can stand up for ourselves without hurting others. We can love and be immovable in our principles at the same time.

True strength is not in whether we stand our ground or not; it is in *how* we stand our ground.

> Honey, get off the cross. Somebody else needs the wood.
>
> —*Dolly Parton*

---

6. The problem with my life? Nobody loves me!

One of the most destructive myths we may use to justify our behavior is the excuse that the rest of the world just does not respect us enough. "People have something against me. People just don't do nice things for me. The problem with love? It's not my love that's the problem. It's everyone else's love. People don't love me enough, and that's the problem... I'm great at love; it's everyone else's deficit of love toward me that's a problem."

This myth leads us into telling ourselves, "I'll start treating people nice when they start treating me nice!" I am sorry, but if we are waiting for all of the world to treat us nice, we will have to wait until the cows come home and the moon turns blue. This is a convenient excuse because we will always be mistreated by someone. It happens to all of us. Jerks are out there. When we use this excuse, we simply have become members of their team.

This irrational way of thinking can be the favorite saying of the Persecuted Jerk (see Step Five), but we have to be careful because we all are capable of having a pity party and a "poor me" moment, and we then gather evidence to support our belief.

We do this because we are feeling sorry for ourselves, and rather than take responsibility for our lack of lovability, we immerse ourselves in whining and self-persecution. If we do this too often, we cannot turn back, and we turn into a Persecuted Jerk.

This myth is generally obvious to outside observers. It is very clear that people are not treating you with much love for the simple reason that you are not very lovable. You have chosen to think and act like an unlovable person. But the bottom line is this: everyone around you will go on loving lovable people, but they will avoid you because you cannot take the risk to drop your guard, drop a little ego, and make yourself more vulnerable. My favorite quote to summarize this is from Robert Anthony, when he said, "Most people would rather be certain they are miserable than risk being happy."

When we are hostile, we are not very lovable. It is risky to drop a shield and become lovable. When we are in this unlovable state of mind, it is obvious to everyone except ourselves. We are not very lovable when we think it is our constitutional right to be loved. We are not very lovable when we are mean to people and then say, "Why don't you love me more?" It does not take a rocket scientist to figure out why we are not receiving love in our lives.

This is one of the most important myths of all because it has such far-reaching implications. It will become a downward spiral that will be our doom if it is not changed. Whenever we are feeling like we need more love, we need to make ourselves more lovable. It is not really that we are doomed to a lonely fate. As Amy Tan once said, "If you can't change your fate, change your attitude."

> Take your life into your own hands, and what happens?
> A terrible thing: no one to blame.
> —Erica Jong

7. I couldn't help it! I wasn't myself.

You were not yourself? Who were you? Charles Manson? Satan?

Not long ago, a pro-athlete was involved in hitting another athlete in the back of the head, then driving the opponent's head into the ground and breaking his neck. His response? "I just wasn't myself." What happened? Did a delinquent criminal crawl into your brain?

This excuse is irrational because we cannot be anyone but ourselves. It is also the ultimate act of human irresponsibility, and worst of all, we are forfeiting the one dignified human trait that no one can ever take from us: our freedom to choose how we want to act in a given situation. When we say, "I couldn't help it. I wasn't myself," we are claiming that there are situations and circumstances in our lives in which we will never be able to think rationally.

> I imagine the reason that people hold on to hatred so stubbornly is because if the hate is removed, the pain will set in.
>
> —*James Baldwin*

8. I'm just kidding! Lighten up and have a sense of humor!

A popular talk show host played a song titled "Barack the Magic Negro," then defended it by saying it was "creative and funny." The song made fun of the first black President of the United States while invoking negative and racist terms.

If both parties are not laughing, then we are laughing at someone else's expense in an effort to dehumanize him. Humanistic psychologist Abraham Maslow noted that self-actualized people have a philosophical and cordial sense of humor, not a hostile one. We tune in to YouTube, and we laugh at stupidity. However, if we use humor to attack someone, we are instigating violence toward the target of our humor. Comedic musical performer Victor Borge summed up sophisticated humor well when he said, "Laughter is the shortest distance between two people." If our form of humor is not bringing people together, it is hostile. A pathological sense of humor takes joy in hurting others. Actually, we are not just being a jerk, we are acting like a racist jerk.

> Hate is sadness wrapped in razors.
>
> —*Aaron French*

9. It's a free country. I can say what I like!

The only true freedom is the freedom to rise above the insanity, not join it. Sometimes our cruel behavior can be a danger to society, but most of the time, we are just being a nuisance. For the record, most jerk-like behavior is not punishable by a court of law. It is not against the law to be annoying, insulting, petty, gossipy, and shallow. We do not go to jail for being the queen of misery, the king of complaints, or the prince of pessimism. These people exist, and we need to learn to live around them without becoming like them or succumbing to their misery and their excuses. Jerks certainly do have the right to speak their mind. However, when that so-called "honest" speech is created for propaganda, slander, or to incite violence against others, it is a crime. We do not have the right to invite harm toward others.

It does not matter whether you are a leader or an average citizen; all of us have the power to influence others. Freedom carries great responsibility. Freedom requires objectivity and reason.

The Internet is a breeding ground for hate. Websites have sprung up throughout the world supporting racist and hateful speech intended not only to demean, but to incite violence. With freedom of speech also comes the knowledge that what we say has the potential to recruit vulnerable people who are looking for reasons to hate. When this hate results in violence, we have violated the fundamental principles of what it means to be free. The hardcore racist does not seek a public debate to decide why one view is more virtuous than others; the cruel person's only goal is to increase hostility against humanity.

On an individual scale, an irresponsible claim to freedom of speech results in children learning how to bring great harm to others with rumors, covert text messages, subversive bullying, slandering, and judgment. The lesson to our youth is that you can say what you want and not be held accountable.

When you overhear your teenage daughter disparage a classmate, you ask, "Where did you learn to be so mean to others?" Often you do not have to look far. Perhaps you are the parent in the front seat listening to rant radio or gossiping about a neighbor. "Hey, it's a free country! I can say what I want!" Yes, you can. But there are consequences for being hostile. You may be raising the next generation of cruel people.

True freedom is the freedom to build humanity. No one has the individual right to destroy humanity.

> We can have peace after we stop hating love and stop loving hate.
>
> —*Josh Hite*

10. I was just giving them a taste of their own medicine! They deserved it! Besides, it's the only thing that these people understand!

The notion of getting even may be one of the most counter-productive personal philosophies we can possess. It shortens our lives by relinquishing a portion of it to hurtful thinking and hurtful behavior. Getting even with others is merely revealing that we are no longer interested in getting along. When we focus on the pain we have experienced, then obsess on how we can pass this pain on to another person, a series of changes occurs in our cognitive functioning. We are no longer adding to the wealth of the world, but adding to its poverty. This is a poverty of thought that results in cycles of irrational thinking. The internal message that justifies cruelty is repeated over and over: "They had it coming! They deserve it! Besides, it's the only thing they understand!" A Hungarian proverb sums up what happens when we give up responsibility: "Do not be cruel to others unless you are willing to be responsible for their acts of cruelty later in life."

We often complain of school violence, and we wonder why these kids act this way. The answer is simple: we have taught them to act this way, and they grow up believing that getting even is a legitimate method of problem solving. We dress it up with cute sayings such as, "I was just giving her a taste of her own medicine. You should know that if you hurt me, I'm going to hurt you back." The major problem with thinking, speaking, and acting this way is that we are creating chains of violations that will never end. If we believe that getting even is admirable, then we are not only condoning, but also teaching violence. In 90% of all acts of school violence, students report they were just getting even. If getting even is part of our personal philosophy, we would approve a person getting even by shooting co-workers, stabbing a classmate, or vandalizing property to settle a feud. Of course, these examples are extreme, but they are a reminder that getting even serves no purpose in teaching peace.

We need to control the dangerous criminals in society to keep everyone safe. In order for any sane society to avoid social anarchy, we need to have a set of rules that are agreed upon by the democratic system. These laws help us feel secure and protected.

When we feel the need to justify our mean behavior, most of the time it is a matter of believing that we have exhausted every other possible solution. It is an indicator that we believe we are above another person. We have made a judgment that the other has an inferior set of deductive skills; therefore, we need the power of violence, cruelty, and fear in order to change him.

The need to control all of the jerks in life often may be the result of comparing ourselves to others. Jealousy is one of the most pathological of all social emotions. "I don't have the right to that fast-moving lane, so why should you? I can't budge in line, so why should you? I can't have affluence, popularity, or success, so why should you?" We are certain that others have something we do not have, and that something is keeping us from our happiness. Thus, we strive to have control over that something, as though this will enhance our happiness.

Do you think that a morning rage-filled commute makes you better at the workplace? It is impossible to rage at the world and come home and stop raging. It carries into marriages, parenting, and personal lives. You cannot be a good dad at home when you are a raging dad on the highway.

There has been a great deal of research to try to understand the conditions in which humans experience the most joy and happiness. In the societies that report the highest level of happiness, one feature is consistently present, and this is the quality of shared care for the society's citizens. In other words, everybody takes care of everybody else. A selfless culture thrives, while a controlling, authoritarian, or caste system always fails to come close to universal contentment. These countries can be filled with technology or have very little technology. Some have warm weather; some have very cold weather. Some are deeply religious; others are not. What distinguishes the contented citizens from the discontented depends on the culture of the contributions to the group, not to the self. Some countries that have the highest levels of taxes also have the highest levels of reported happiness. It is because the taxes are seen as a contribution to the greater good, taking care of the elderly, sickly, disabled, and less fortunate. The social programs are far-reaching and remove the stressful burden of wondering how we can take care of ourselves. In other countries, however, these contributions are viewed as subversive influences.

Everyone has had moments of comparing themselves to others. We are trying to experience what we perceive to be the happiness of others. We develop a hoarding mentality and a need to challenge others' abilities to have what we do not have. "How dare you occupy my space of happiness (a better place in line). How dare you occupy a better body of happiness (damn those people on the cover of those magazines—they are so good looking! Isn't it in the Constitution somewhere that everyone has the right to bear six-pack abdominal muscles?). How dare you own my possessions of happiness (I would be so much happier with her clothes and his super cellphone!)."

If we consider what we are doing to ourselves, we may realize what an incredible waste of time it is to ponder such issues.

The bigger question is: what happened to the happy gene, and how did it get replaced with the misery gene? There was a documentary about a tropical island that was regarded with awe by visitors. People returned and commented on how the society was so happy. Is it possible to be happy all the time, smile every day, and have few or no possessions and property?

What's the key? It is simple if we open our eyes. The happiest people on earth spend little time comparing themselves to others. In other societies, this comparison is a national pastime! The tabloids would go out of business if they could not do this!

When we compare ourselves to no one, there is no measuring stick for a rich life. When wealth is internally measured, it is externally manifested through laughter and smiles. When we are very wealthy in spirit (with an internal sense of joy, love, and freedom), we will find it much more difficult to engage in external behaviors that compromise our integrity.

There is also less of a need constantly to seek new environments to increase one's personal joy. I have no desire to move to the highly-taxed country or the tropical island because I like my present environment. I like what my living conditions have to offer. I like my job, my opportunities, and the people around me. Sometimes we have to change environments (move away from an abusive relationship, quit working for the tyrant boss, or move to weather better suited for our health), but most of the time, we have to realize that life will have its inherent difficulties, stressors, and jerks, and our job is not to conquer them, but to coexist with them peacefully.

There are times when it is important to try to experience others' lives, and this is when we are trying to ease their pain. When we are empathetic and compassionate toward the poor, victims of violence, victims of natural disaster, and those afflicted by disease, we seek to ease their pain.

When we try to place ourselves in the shoes of those of whom we are jealous, we are trying to figure out what they have that would create our happiness. We look at others and say, "Wow! The *Fortune 500* list! That must be the key to happiness!" But what if all of the people in the top 100 were all taking medication for panic attacks, and they were in therapy for depression? Would you still want to be them? "Ah, but I would know how to handle their wealth. Unlike them, I would be happy with their possessions." Sooner or later we have to face this fundamental insight: outside of basic survival needs, no one else's stuff will make us happy. When we are jealous for others' stuff, we forget what we already have. We are unable to absorb or be grateful for our own sunshine, blue sky, fresh air, laughter, friendships, love, family, children's activities, elementary school plays, human warmth, sights, senses (eyesight, mobility, hearing, touch), health, or most importantly, time on this earth. Our time on earth is the one thing that cannot be harvested, re-generated, or created. Why waste it in the miserable and futile exercise of trying to generate control over others? We need to put our energy into cooperation with others, in which we can contribute to collaboration, democracy, sane laws, acceptance of differences, and a town hall that can include all inhabitants on earth.

Step Four:

Embracing the Eight Habits of Thinking of the Jerk Whisperer

> Finish each day and be done with it. You have done what you could; some blunders and absurdities have crept in; forget them as soon as you can. Tomorrow is a new day; you shall begin it serenely and with too high a spirit to be encumbered with your old nonsense.
>
> *—Ralph Waldo Emerson*

1. Find your flow

Today's world is filled with more available information than at any other point in human history. This saturation of electronic data allows us to text, talk, communicate via satellite, and drive our cars at the same time. We use terms like multi-task to fool ourselves into thinking that we can do a lot of things at the same time. Much of the time, we believe we need to speed up to keep up. Speeding up is the most destructive thing we can do. When we speed up, the only thing we are speeding toward is an early death.

An important habit for a jerk whisperer is to do one thing at a time, and do that thing in a controlled, focused manner. You cannot arm-wrestle Mother Nature. She will not only win, she will break your arm.

Many years ago, I had the great honor of studying with a professor by the name of Dr. Richard Bear. He was a gentle man who often shared his American Indian philosophy when he saw us (doctoral grad students) experiencing unnecessary stress in our lives. One day I was overwhelmed with papers, assignments, exams, and family responsibilities when he stopped me and asked, "Steve, how fast is the river moving today?" I will never forget his words because they still resonate with me. Dr. Bear passed away a few years ago, but his beauty had an everlasting effect on so many of us.

His words were a simple reminder that life can only move so fast. No matter how hard we fight, we are no match for the river. We may lag behind because we cannot keep up, or we may try to swim faster than the current to arrive sooner. In either case, we are fighting the current, and we will be exhausted when this leg of the journey ends. Thus, Dr. Bear's philosophy was to look at each day's river, determine how fast it is moving, and find a way to stay with the current.

The quote on the previous page by Ralph Waldo Emerson is also an eloquent arrangement of thoughts to capture beautifully the essence of a centered philosophy. We need to strive to stay in the moment, and this striving begins with the art of staying in day-tight compartments. Mr. Emerson suggests that we put things behind us in spite of our mistakes and start each day anew. Most of us realize that we are being irrational when we dwell on absurdities and carry them into the next day.

In order to stay with the flow of life, we cannot keep dropping yesterday's obstacles in the path of today's course. Otherwise, as we negotiate today's river, we will spend a lot of energy paddling around yesterday's insane unfinished issues.

It is impossible to take a minute's time and magically extend it to 70 seconds. It is impossible to put 25 hours into a 24-hour day, or put an extra two days into a month. Nature only goes at one speed, and no one has been able to defy this fact. The secret is not to change nature, but to find our place within it. Ralph Waldo Emerson also said, "Adopt the pace of nature: her secret is patience."

Happy, well-adjusted, calm people do not really think of this as a secret; they already know the futility of impatience, multitasking, and overscheduling. They do not fight the river. Your river may be work tasks, long lines, traffic, or family. Float with the current; drop the ego. No single person in the history of humankind has conquered the river. Admit to yourself that you will not be the first.

What is the evidence that you have found your flow in life? You can laugh at the little stressors and move on. Find your flow.

> Take the time to come home to yourself everyday.
> —*Robin Cesarjean*

2. Be mindful

In a moment, you will need to stop and ponder a question. Be as honest as you can, be as objective as you can, and think for at least a couple of minutes before you come to your conclusion. Read the following question, then place your book down for a minute to ponder your answer.

The question is this: In an average day, what percentage of people in your world would you consider to be jerks? Think about the day in its entirety, from the moment you wake until the moment you fall asleep. Consider neighbors, friends, other drivers, family, other shoppers, clerks, waiters, loved ones, and co-workers. Consider everyone. Then assign a percentage to this group of people—90%? 50%? 20%? 10%? Use your own definition. (Do not say, "Well, it depends on what you mean by a jerk.") However you define a jerk, use that definition and come up with a figure, then put your book down for a minute and come to your conclusion.

In your opinion, what percentage of the people in your world are jerks?

As I do workshops with people all over the country, I often ask this question. The "percent of jerks" question is very important because our answers reveal more about how we see the world than what it actually is. Sometimes people are convinced that, "You would see more jerks in this world if you had to spend more time in my shoes!"

For the record, my shoes are a size 4. I am only 4'8" tall, and if I had to spend time in your shoes, I would probably trip a lot. And if you had to spend time in my shoes, your feet would probably hurt. But nonetheless, let me tell you about my shoes. I am a short, little man. I have graying chin whiskers that I wear in a beard or goatee, and I have a deeper voice than most people my height. Every day of my life, I turn people's heads. Kids run up to me in a supermarket and inquire if I'm an elf, people take an extra look at me, and sometimes I sense others' discomfort as they feel compelled to lean down, squat, or sit when they are speaking to me. My roommate in college said that one of his favorite things to do was to walk behind me a few steps everywhere we went because he got a kick out of watching people do a double-take or stare at me (he was one of those people who is tall—and he played on the college basketball team). When I speak to schools on nonviolence and bullying, I often have a question and answer period at the end. Ninety percent of the time, the first question is, "How tall is your wife?" Annie is only 5'4", but I tell them she is 6'1" just to see their reaction.

My shoes are my shoes. I cannot swap them. I laugh like heck when a four year-old kid gets excited to tell his mom, "There's an elf in the cereal aisle!" Are these kids jerks? No, they are wonderful, smart, observant, and curious.

So what percent of people in your day are jerks? The real answer to the question is another question itself: Speaking from the view of being in my shoes, what percentage of people in this world do I perceive to be jerks?

When I speak at conferences and workshops, I've had people shout out their percentages. I am often amazed at their answers, and I wonder what it must be like to live in the hell they call "their shoes." They say, "90% of the people in my world are jerks! You should see my coworkers! 60%! You should see my morning commute! 40%! You should meet my family! 70%! You should live around my neighbors!" I've even heard people claim, "Everyone I work with is a jerk!"

If everyone you work with is a jerk, you need to re-evaluate your life. If your percentage is more than 10%, I encourage you to re-evaluate your life. I believe that the jerks are less than 1% percent of the world. They get a lot more attention than they deserve, and they get all the headlines. But if we really open our eyes, we will see a world that is filled with wonderful people everywhere we go. If it seems like everyone around you is a jerk, you may want to ask yourself what you are doing to bring that out in them.

Many years ago I had a co-worker complain about every place he had worked: "It seems like everywhere I work, I end up with a lot of people who are out to get me! This is the fifth job in a row where people have filed complaints against me!" I told him, "What a shame. I must be lucky. Everywhere I work, they treat me like I'm royalty! People seem to go out of their way to be helpful to me!"

If it seems like you are receiving more than your fair share of mistreatment, it is not because you are cursed; it is more likely that you are creating a cursed lifestyle. We create responses in others. When we approach people with a particular attitude, they often will return it. Happy approach? Happy response. Demanding, entitled approach? Stonewall response. Respectful approach? Respectful response.

Being mindful is an attitude, tone, and intention. Often people will use a sweet voice and believe they are being civil. You can use a sweet voice and still act like a jerk. You have just dressed up your approach as if to say, "No one could possibly be as sweet as me!"

If you believe that 90% of the people you work with or 90% of the people on the road are jerks, there is a danger that your attitude will bleed into all areas of your life. You then start to develop a defensive, negative attitude that carries into your family life, love life, and personal life. You take the attitude of a road rager, inherit it, and bring it home to your loved ones.

Before you know it, this mindlessness leads to misery and self-persecution as you start to believe you are a victim. We can be victims of discrimination (for the record, as a short person, I can reach only about half the things on the shelves in an average supermarket). However, I really don't feel as though most of the world is miserable. The world does not always fit my needs, but I believe that the percentage of true jerks in this world is very small.

I have a wonderful friend who is a school counselor in a "low-performing" school in California. (I have a problem with the term *low-performing* school—it should be called an *inadequately resourced* school because these schools are never the ones with high socioeconomic conditions. *Low-performing* often has more to do with poverty than it does with lazy teachers and lazy kids, but that is another rant for another day.) This counselor, whom I will call Ms. Lucero, is a wonderful, selfless, dedicated educator. You easily can detect her dedication and investment in her students by the way she describes them. Whenever she refers to a really tough, oppositional kid, she says how bad she feels because this kid was damaged somewhere along the way. Miserable educators have a lot of "bad kids." Ms. Lucero has never had a "bad kid." She considers her students disconnected, and she puts all of her efforts into establishing trust and reconnecting with them. As a result, she is seen by her peers as a gifted educator. Her gift is her ability to see the good in others rather than the bad.

Oppositional children, as well as oppositional adults, have had their connections damaged. As a result, they are operating with damaged wiring.

Another psychologist I worked with several years ago referred to his clients as battered kittens. He worked with some of the most difficult borderline, paranoid, histrionic, and antisocial personality disorders. When asked, "How can you work with these people day after day?" his response was, "Nothing rips your heart out like a battered kitten. It's like your heart falls out of your chest when you see this cold, shivering, battered kitten on the side of the road. In so many cases, they grow up to be big ugly cats, but I always like to see them in my mind as the battered kitten left on the side of the road. Even big ugly cats can live in harmony with others, if given the chance."

What is the evidence that you are mindful in life? You can laugh at your own mindlessness, and the mindlessness of others and realize that there is a small percentage of full-time jerks in the world. Find your flow, and be mindful.

> Twenty years from now you will be more
> disappointed by the things you didn't do than by the
> ones you did. Throw off the bowlines. Sail away
> from your safe harbor. Catch the trade winds in
> your sails. Explore. Dream. Discover.
>
> —Mark Twain

3. Get out of your own way

Mark Twain said it well when he said, "Sail away from your safe harbor." We can get caught up in our own little habits and make a million excuses for being rigid, but the price we pay is steep. We waste our lives and never explore ourselves; we never really dream, and we lose every opportunity to discover.

There are two important steps we need to take in order to get out of our own way. First, focus on real problems. We have witnessed incredibly real problems in our lives. Losing loved ones, war, natural disasters, illness, and accidents are real problems. Spilling your drink in the back seat of a car is not a crisis, nor is it an emergency. Being late for a movie is not a crisis, nor is it the end of the world. Getting cut off in traffic is not a crisis, nor is it a reason to risk your life trying to get revenge on the perpetrator. Waiting in line for groceries is not a crisis; imagine having no food—even for one day. Forgetting to record your favorite show is not a crisis; it's just another example of life not going as perfectly as planned.

Many of life's crises are imagined and invented. They are the ones ricocheting around in our skulls. I heard some great advice some time ago from a psychologist who suggested that we should avoid having the same thought twice unless that thought is enjoyable. The problem is that we repeat negative thoughts over and over and fail to repeat our positive thoughts.

All of us know that person who has an uncanny ability to turn any minor change in his life into a crisis. "Can you believe they are taking out three spaces in our parking lot! Oh my! Can you believe they changed the policy on leaving work early? Oh my! Can you believe we now have to pay more for a stamp? Oh my!"

My response is: "Can you believe I just lost a full minute of my life listening to you talk about this garbage? And I will never get that minute back!"

I call these people petty-philes. They are obsessed with the petty, and they put so much energy into ludicrous issues. For instance, there was a recent political election when a candidate was asked by a member of the media why he was not wearing a little flag pin on his suit like the other candidate. The press blew it out of proportion and tried to connect it to a lack of patriotism. The candidate addressed the issue with dignity and took the gentle, politically correct approach. For just one moment I would have liked to have seen him simply fire back with a commonsense response: "What in heaven's name is wrong with you? Are you really going to waste a portion of your life thinking about a tiny pin? Today a mother lost her son in an insane war; today a child died of starvation as his brothers and sisters wept; today we irreparably destroyed another portion of our ozone layer; today a man made one dollar in wages to make your plasma TV…and you are obsessed with a tiny pin? What is rotting in that space you call a brain?"

Of course, you will have the person who will claim that the symbolism of a tiny flag pin shows you are a true patriot, but I disagree. There are despicable people who wave flags and carry their holy books and treat others in horrible ways. The real evidence is in doing what is right, not talking about it. The real evidence is not in a tiny flag symbol, but perhaps doing things that actually preserve liberty.

We need to stop making crises where they do not exist. When we do, we realize that we can create personal lives that are virtually crisis-less. By focusing on real problems, we can avoid the petty-philes, be grateful for what we have, and become more of an appreciator than a critic.

I do not think that the people who were focusing on the pin really understood suffering in this world. Paul Smith once said, "Those who have suffered understand suffering and therefore extend their hand."

If we ever lose our gratefulness, we also lose our ability to find the miracles in life. Life is full of miracles! Albert Einstein once said, "There are only two ways to live your life. One is as though nothing is a miracle. The other is as though everything is a miracle." I love finding and believing in all the miracles in life—it's so much more fun!

The second step to getting out of our own way is to "utilize life time." We do this by developing a 90/10 lifestyle. We create our own roadblocks by unnecessarily carrying them around with us. Throughout the day, there are situations, people, and chance occurrences that have the potential to be stressful. But if I spend five extra minutes in a line, why should I let it ruin the next three hours? If I have to spend thirty minutes in a meeting with a narcissistic rantaholic (a person who is so self-absorbed he becomes addicted to rants), why should I let him occupy my thoughts beyond those thirty minutes?

The key is the 90/10 way of thinking. What do you need to survive in a day's time? Are you concerned that you may not eat today? Then maybe half of your day should be spent thinking about how you will get today's food. The same would hold true if you were concerned about freezing to death, or if you may be apprehended because you spoke out with a political view, or if you were in a critical life-or-death situation.

But some of the most miserable people on earth have few real problems and spend 80-90% of their day consumed in miserable thought. If you leave your problems in the timeframe in which they occurred, you find that about 90% of your day has the potential to be productive, enjoyable, and stress-free. A 90/10 philosophy is letting the 10% of your day stay right where it is. Quarantine your poisons. Leave them in your boss's office, in the traffic jam, in the discussion with your crazy neighbor, or in the doctor's office. Do not let them bleed into your productive time, your loving time, your friendship time, dinnertime, or your walk around your neighborhood.

Ralph Waldo Emerson said, "Grow angry slowly; there's plenty of time." We cannot be so quick as to deem every stressor as capable of ruining our day. What is the evidence that we have a 90/10 philosophy? You have had a day that by far has had all the love, laughs, and goodwill shared and spent before your head hits the pillow.

What is the evidence that you can get out of your own way? You can look in the mirror, see your own faults, and laugh as you realize that life is a great big joke, and you are the punchline.

Find your flow, be mindful, and get out of your own way.

> When we hate our enemies, we are giving them happiness. Our enemies would dance with joy if only they knew how they were worrying us, lacerating us, and getting even with us! Our hate is not hurting them at all, but our hate is turning our days and nights into a hellish turmoil.
>
> —*Dale Carnegie*

4. Don't hate the hateful

When we stop to think about issues of hate, we realize that hate is simply unreasonable. We need to find reason in unreasonable situations. This is not to say that we should never be angry. Anger can be reasonable, but to induce hate is to let the anger fester into a painful sore that constantly brings us pain. Aristotle summed up the issue of anger nicely when he said, "Anyone can become angry. That is easy. But to be angry with the right person, to the right degree, at the right time, for the right purpose and in the right way—that is not easy."

When we hate criminals, we take on their worst quality. When we become hateful because someone does not live his life according to our standards, morals, or beliefs, we have swapped our potential for growth for a potential for destruction.

When we hate the hateful, we become like them. The only way to deal with this is to forgive and let it go. What is the evidence that you can let go of your hate? You can let people be themselves (which allows each of us to be more of ourselves), laugh, and move on. You can learn to change others through education and teachable moments rather than pursuing the need to crush, fight, and bomb your perceived enemy.

Buddha once said, "Never in the world does hatred cease by hatred; hatred ceases by love. Let us live most happily, free from hatred in the midst of the hateful."

Find your flow, be mindful, get out of your own way, and don't hate the hateful.

We need to spend less of life trying to prove others wrong and more of life learning what is right.

5. Be in control—but not a controller

Often, I speak to thousands of people at conferences and corporate meetings, but sometimes out of the blue I get an invitation to speak to very small groups. Not long ago I spoke to a wonderful group of people at a small-town library about an hour away from where I live. There were only a few dozen people who arrived at the library on that wintry evening. The library was located in the basement of an office building. The small town of 200 citizens had a tiny library, and they were very proud of all it had to offer. The displays of children's drawings, poetry, announcements, and bulletin boards revealed that pride. The library had a lot of children's books, a handful of best sellers, and all of the classics. Several people in the town had read my book and wanted to talk about it.

After I had made a short presentation, an elderly man approached me and said, "Dr. Bird, you may not remember me, but I was sitting in the audience a few years ago. I am a retired bus driver, and after we finished our routes on that morning, you were our guest speaker, and you talked about how we can work toward better connections with kids. I wanted to be here tonight because I wanted to tell you that my life changed that morning. What I remember most was realizing that I, and only I, am responsible for my attitude. I was miserable, and I was blaming the kids for my misery, I was blaming my home life, and sadly, I was blaming my loved ones. I am ashamed to admit that it took me this long in life to realize something so small but so important. After that day, I realized that I am responsible for my attitude."

The man gave me a teary hug, but I will never forget him, and I have never overlooked the power of a few words when it comes to supporting one another. I had no idea that a short talk on how to connect better to kids, in a bus garage, to a group of bus drivers, on a snowy morning could reverberate in this way years later.

I thanked the man for his kind words, and I appreciated the reminder that I too was the only one responsible for my control in life. I often talk to so many groups, and I wonder if I make any difference. Does my message get through to anyone? Did I help at least one person to realize that he does not need to snap at his loved ones, mistreat people at his job, or curse the world? I realize that all I can do is be me. I cannot control anyone except myself. That exchange also reminded me of the words of the English novelist from the 1800s, George Eliot, who said, "It's never too late to be who you might have been."

Control with others means giving up control. Social theories and counseling theories on human groups reveal one thing that is abundantly clear about all groups: we cannot have complete control over everything in life, but we can control our reactions to things.

Every person belongs to groups. These can be a small group of two (loving relationships), small groups of everyday relationships (co-workers, neighbors), or large groups (crowded malls, highways, cities). The only way to maintain our sanity in these groups is to do two things. First, be responsible for your own attitude. And second, be okay with not being able to have your way always.

The beauty of any long-lasting relationship is that you have given up a little external control in order to let a little wisdom in. For instance, if you have been in a relationship for twenty years and you still have love for that other person, you have both let each other's little things slide. You have to be okay if one of you likes pizza and the other does not. You have to be okay with one of you being a "morning person" when the other is not. The list can go on and on, but the common dynamic of long-lasting relationships is reciprocal respect—you let others be who they are. They may be different, but if they are not hurting you, let it go.

Sometimes we adapt, and these differences can become a wonderful part of the "us." I have been an early riser my entire life (it goes back to my paperboy delivery days). I wake up every day before my wife. Since I am up early, I bring her a cup of coffee and place it on her nightstand. She tells me that it makes her day. Sometimes she still has her head on the pillow, and when I see the dimple that comes with her smile, it makes my day too. We are different, and it works.

When it comes to differences, the same holds true for working with the same people year after year. If you constantly cannot get past your petty obsessions, you will lose your sanity. It also applies to neighbors, urban living, political views, and all of life's conditions. Give up a little control of the external things, but hold steadfast to your internal control. The happiest people on earth have mastered this way of thinking. They have removed the need to control others. They can give up control without being oppressed. Oppression is unhealthy for anyone, and in such cases, you have to change the scene or get out of the scene, relationship, or job.

When people are paranoid and feel threatened by others living a lifestyle they desire, there is a strong possibility that they have fed themselves a steady diet of self-pity, which results in the belief that everyone is unfair to them. For example, I once heard a miserable writer say, "The publishers just won't give me a chance!" My response is, "So what! Get over yourself, write anyway! Write for the beauty of the writing. Stop the self-persecution, and enjoy the process!" Whatever you choose to do in life, find your reasons for enjoying it.

We also see examples of people who take their petty obsessions to another level and seek to terrorize others with their views. I know a wonderful woman who lives in California. She is a dedicated, decent, law-abiding teacher. She has never broken the law and gives selflessly to her community. She lives with her wife, who is also a wonderful, kind person. They are legally married, and they live in the suburbs. When California citizens were voting in an attempt to ban same-sex marriages, some of the neighbors went out of their way to plant signs against such rights around their house. The couple said they felt as if they were in Nazi Germany with the Gestapo putting signs up on Jewish homes and businesses, all for the purpose of hate.

Whatever your view may be on same-sex marriage, does it not make sense to ask yourself, "Aren't there bigger fish to fry in this world? Do we not have more important issues to dwell upon?" These people are not breaking any laws, and they live their lives without harming anyone. They make the world a better place, contribute to their society, and they are married because they have found love. Does it not make more sense to put your efforts into bigger issues? There are hundreds of issues of greater importance than this narrow interpretation of how people should live. What about the corporate giant who has stolen millions of dollars from innocent people? Or the pedophiles, drug-induced crimes, domestic abuse, random acts of violence, or sexual predators on the Internet? Why attack law-abiding citizens? This kind of fanaticism is born of fear and perpetuated by paranoia. This is the same fanaticism that maintained slavery, segregation, and insisted that women were second-class citizens and should never be allowed to vote.

What is the evidence that you can let go of your need to control? It's this: you can respect and enjoy others' differences; you can enjoy yourself in spite of not being able to control every situation and every conversation; you can laugh when you have that silly need to be in control; you realize that those who strive for the most control on the outside often feel the most out of control on the inside.

Find your flow, be mindful, get out of your own way, don't hate the hateful, and be in control.

> You can't solve a problem if it's not your own.
> —*Brooke Bolen*

6. Be a role model, not a reform model

Role models set examples. Reform models impose themselves on others. Reform models obsess on others' behaviors rather than their own. If you need to count the minutes you spend on a task in your office and then compare to other workers' amount of work, you are obsessing on the wrong things in life. If you find that you constantly need to be the line cop in the supermarket "She was here before you, and I was here before her, and he was here first...") you probably are obsessing on the wrong things. If you are counting items in others' baskets, slowing down on the highway to control others, and noting the exact time that other coworkers arrive and leave, you are obsessing on the wrong things.

If you are trying to be judge and jury for every act you deem wrong, and feel the need to "teach everybody a lesson," you are trying to be a reform model instead of a role model. Pretty soon you will feel so overwhelmed with these preoccupations that you will not be able to sleep at night or enjoy simple pleasures.

The quote on the previous page from Brooke Bolen, "You can't solve a problem if it's not your own," was actually spoken in a college counseling class in which I was teaching. One person in the group was rambling on about how he needed to change his mother-in-law, straighten out his neighbor, tell off his uncle, and get his spouse in line, and he also went on to mention that all of these people were making his life crazy. After the rant, a very small, soft-spoken woman (Brooke) said, "You can't solve a problem if it's not your own." It was so simple and so succinctly stated that it struck a chord with everyone in the group.

There is so much to reflect upon from this simple statement. The bottom line? You have made their problem yours, and you did not need to. The greater problem occurs when you believe that you have the right to correct everyone's behavior and obsess on how you need to reform the world.

We need to live by our values and for our values, not for an insane belief that we need to reform everyone. Religious fanatics can abuse their personal relationship with God by insisting that their God has given them the right not just to believe a certain way, but to invade other people's worlds, condemn them, and make their lives miserable if they are not living up to their standards. These people are filled with hatred, unrest, and hostility and hide behind a deity to condone their need to upset others. We have extreme terrorists who blow up others because they believe God wants them to use physical force to reform them, and we have verbal terrorists who stand on street corners, invade our office space, and overtly invade others' lives. We have moral terrorists who want to preach endlessly about our habits and our lack of goodness if a person decides to indulge in any behavior that appears wrong or weak in their eyes.

These people become so obsessed with the behavior of others that they fail to see how they are violating others' rights to have peaceful lives. It is a travesty when people in influential positions abuse their power to point out the mistakes of others. Some time ago, when my son was in college, he had a class with an abusive professor. The professor decided to humiliate a student in front of the class because she had read the course syllabus incorrectly and would be late in handing in her assignment. The professor said, "It looks like some of us don't pay attention very well, and one of us may not be passing the class." The student left the class in tears. My son, like several other students, was obsessed with the idea of making this professor pay for this hideous act (there are a lot of websites to rate your professor these days). We discussed the issue at length, and eventually my son cooled down and decided to take the more difficult road. We talked about how easy it would be to be the punisher, but in the end, who would benefit? Eventually my son came to the conclusion, "It would be a waste of time to be obsessed with reforming this person. I suppose if I really lived by my values, the greatest lesson I could teach myself is to commit to never acting like him." He decided to let this person's insanity be his life lesson—to be a great teacher of compassion, not cruelty. It hurt him to see a fellow student hurt by an egotist, and now he had to make up his mind about what kind of values he would exercise in his own life. His decision was not to take on the role of the reform model (like the professor), but to remain true to his values by becoming a role model.

Another example of this happened to me recently as I was driving to work. I stopped at an intersection, I looked both ways, and the closest car was about 500 yards away. After I pulled onto the highway, I noticed that the car sped up extremely fast and rode on my bumper for the next three miles. Eventually another car came between us, and I didn't see the insane driver again…until thirty minutes later. I was at a gas station, and I heard a voice behind me say, "You need to stop pulling out in front of people on the highway!" I was startled, and I said, "I'm sorry, what happened?"

"You pulled your car out in front of me!"

I then recognized the car. It was the insane person who had ridden my bumper. I asked, "You followed me all the way to this gas station to tell me that?"

"Yes! You need to stop pulling out in front of people!"

I ended the discussion by trying to calm her down and re-assure her that nothing was intentional. I also was frightened. She was a reform model, attempting to reform the world and punish anyone who violated her rules. These are the people who run others off the road and sometimes take their irrational behavior to another level and hurt others.

I tried to imagine what her day must be like. She most likely is filled with petty obsessions as she dwells on how she can try to change the world to fit her needs. To dwell for thirty minutes on the little professor who pulled into traffic and did not abide by her rules is simply a waste of life. Do you have no more important things to dwell upon? Could your energies be channeled in better directions—perhaps thoughts of love, grate-fulness, or simple appreciation for the gift of life today?

Reform models abuse power. Role models share their pow-er, joy, and energy with others. Role models are teachers; re-form models are punishers. What is the evidence that you are a role model and not a reform model? You can let go of the need to punish and change everyone whom you may cross paths with, you can laugh at how nutty you have been when you do this, and most importantly, you have exercised your power to move on.

Find your flow, be mindful, get out of your own way, don't hate the hateful, be in control, and be a role model.

Ultimately, love is self-approval.

—*Sondra Ray*

---

7. Love yourself in a selfless way

Imagine a friend of yours coming up to you and saying, "Hey friend, I would like you to meet Ernie. I'm also going to ask you to love Ernie. I really need you to love Ernie with all your heart. By the way, friend, I hate Ernie. In fact, I despise him."

If your friend had this conversation with you, you would think he or she was crazy! My goodness, she wants me to love Ernie, but she hates Ernie? What kind of nutty request is that?

As crazy as it sounds, many of us are making this request daily. It's just that the person we want others to love is us. We often have self-loathing, and we still want others to love us. It is impossible to receive love from others when we do not have it for ourselves. If we do not like ourselves, how can we possibly expect others to like us? It also makes sense that we cannot teach something or give something away that we do not have. If we do not have love, we cannot give it away.

A lack of self-love is also a unique form of isolation. When we are dismayed at why we are distancing ourselves from other people, we are often at odds with the person in the mirror. We then end up blaming others for not loving us enough, but the bottom line is that we have decided for ourselves that we are unlovable or do not deserve any better. When we do not love ourselves, we push others away. We become unhuggable, frowning, and unlovable persons.

Self-loving people constantly feed themselves a meaningful life because they are looking for a spark in their exchanges with others. They are proud of their kindness, courtesy, and civility and take pride in how they can share that with others, smile at others, give a kind word to others, and somehow, in their efforts, they generate a smile in return. It is that spark that confirms their self-worth and their need to be genuine.

The unlovable part of our everyday thinking became very clear to me in a graduate college course I teach in group counseling. In this course, we have an experiential component in which students volunteer to be part of an actual group therapy process. We change leadership roles each week, and the students take turns leading the group. In one particular week, two of the students led an activity in which we were all given styrofoam cups. We were told that the cup represented our self-worth, and we were to take a pencil and poke holes in it. Each hole represented the things that drain our self-worth. We then processed the activity, and the group members talked about such things as bad habits, unmet goals, and our unlovable qualities. One of the most interesting outcomes of the activity was that every single member of the group mentioned their bodies. Every single member did not like their diets or lack of exercise or extra pounds or big thighs. I was one of them. It then became a rather moving experience when one group member, a lovely woman in her mid-forties, stopped and said, "My goodness, listen to us! Look around! Surely we can all use a little progress on our health, but would you stop and look at us? All I see are a lot of beautiful, loving people. What are we doing to ourselves?"

She was right. I was impressed with every one of these students. They were smart, educated, dedicated, hard-working, generous, beautiful people. In fact, in terms of appearances, all of them looked healthy to me, and half of them looked thin! In spite of this, not a single person was capable of complete self-love, yet we all deserved it. It was evidence of how we have programmed ourselves to pick out our faults and dwell on them, and in the process, we lose a little bit of our potential and a little bit of our self-worth. We keep our beauty from others because of our self-loathing.

The important kind of self-love is not the narcissistic egotist who stands in front of the mirror saying, "Damn, would you look at that beauty!" The healthy kind of self-love is the kind in which we appreciate who we are. There is no point in spending years hating our monster thighs. It is a waste of energy. There is no point in hating ourselves when we get nervous in front of crowds, or forget things, or cannot ever seem to organize our office well enough. This is a waste of our lifetime, and we will never get it back.

We can work on these things without hating ourselves. Some are physical, some are psychological, and some have to do with our level of compatibility. No single person can conquer every goal, achieve every life task, get along with every individual, or fulfill every dream. So what; we need to get over it and appreciate our journey. We can spend our lifetime pointing out all of our flaws and hating them, but it is such a waste of potential.

There is a lot of fascinating research that suggests that we can physically restructure our brains by nurturing pleasurable relationships. It does not matter whether you are fostering that spark between you and a newborn, or friend, or coworker, or even the everyday exchange with the clerk at the store. Our brains actually change when we nurture and stimulate pleasure centers. It is as though we are training the brain to become addicted to the pleasure in healthy relationships. It feels good to love and to validate others. In much the same way, we know that the brain changes when we are depressed; brain activity spirals into an ineffective pattern, and we actually have unproductive and ineffective cognitive functioning. By appreciating ourselves, we appreciate others, and we spiral upwards instead of downwards. Self-love can be a built-in antidepressant!

Appreciate yourself because you cannot give something you do not have. At the very least, be thankful you are not one of the mean jerks in the world! The more you love yourself, the more you will generate energy and light up a room.

What is the evidence that you can love yourself? You can look in the mirror, see your pimples, crooked nose, gray hair, and ever-changing thighs, and still love yourself. You enter a room and people say, "Hey! There's Elizabeth!" and you notice that they light up when they see you. You pass others, and you see them smile and say, "Hi Erica, great to see you!"

If you are passing people or entering rooms and you get a different response, "Oh gads. Here comes Willy...", maybe it is time to start loving yourself a little more.

Find your flow, be mindful, get out of your own way, don't hate the hateful, be in control, be a role model, and love yourself.

> Psychiatry tells us that one out of every five people is completely disturbed. And the reason is that the other four are nuts.
>
> —*Dave Astor*

8. Be a happy nut instead of a miserable nut

The final habit of thinking is a simple philosophy for living. It also may be the most important, and it is the decision to be happy. You do not have to be perfect, life does not have to be perfect, others do not have to be perfect, the weather does not have to be perfect, the traffic does not have to be perfect, and the world does not have to be perfect in order for you to be happy today. You can have gray hair, wrinkles, drooping body parts, bags under your eyes, and less-than-perfect thighs and still be happy. It all comes down to a personal decision.

I already know I am nuts. I have known this for a long time, and I do not try to fool myself. I get stressed, anxious, obsessed, and distracted. Often, I do not sleep well because I cannot shut down my busy brain. I believe I am a typical normal-neurotic. I worry about my loved ones, and I want to keep moving forward. I worry about my parents, and I worry about my children. I go nuts when my baseball team wins, and I go nuts when they lose. In the end, I am a happy nut.

It is entirely possible to be a little neurotic and have a great time in life. It boils down to this: instead of avoiding life's challenges, take them on (it is better to do things crazy, afraid, or hesitant, than not at all). Happiness is a decision, not a condition of life. Happiness is a frame of mind, not a condition of luck. I believe I am very fortunate for all the opportunities that life has afforded, but I am not lucky. If I were lucky, I would have won the lottery by now. I am nothing more and nothing less than a happy nut. Since I already know I am nuts, I decided I would much rather be a happy nut than a miserable nut.

When we decide to be a happy nut, we are creating instant wealth. Miserable people are poor. They may have a lot of money or gadgets, but they lack the affluence that truly makes their life richer—this is emotional affluence. Peaceful, content people can be happy even when they are hungry, live in a trailer, or cannot pay all their bills. Emotional affluence is a habit of thinking that enables people to see their blessings, count their blessings, and make the most of every living moment. Whenever you have opportunity, you have great potential for this emotional affluence. If you live in a country where you can be legally abused because you are a woman, or executed because of your religion, or kept in poverty because of a lack of democracy, you have very few opportunities. If you have to live under these conditions, emotional affluence is much more difficult to obtain. But many miserable people I know live in a world of opportunity, and it is only their attitude that keeps them in emotional poverty, not their circumstances.

What's the evidence that you are a happy nut? Miserable nuts cannot laugh at themselves, love themselves, or live with flaws in themselves or others. Happy nuts can be profoundly flawed and still be deeply passionate about life, love, important causes, and the pursuit of joy.

A happy nut can trip on the carpet and laugh at him- or herself instead of cursing the carpet. The carpet is imperfect, and so are you.

- **Find your flow.**
- **Be mindful.**
- **Get out of your own way.**
- **Don't hate the hateful.**
- **Be in control—but not a controller.**
- **Be a role model, not a reform model.**
- **Love yourself in a selfless way.**
- **Be a happy nut instead of a miserable nut.**

Have these things, be these things, and do these things because you deserve it, and have fun as a happy nut.

Step Five:

Understanding Your Jerk

Who are these jerks anyway?
Four major differences
between the cruel and the kind

The research involving violence in human beings has identified many differences between aggressive and peaceful people. These differences are the same ones found between happy and miserable people because the miserable people also seem to be the ones doing all the attacking. Four characteristics seem to be present in jerks—those who most often violate others.

The *first* difference has to do with impulse control. Cruel people cannot stop themselves from lashing out at others. This quality is independent of age, intellect, or experience. Sometimes this is confused with social inappropriateness. People can be socially inappropriate, perhaps out of naivety, and say the wrong thing at the wrong time; they may embarrass themselves or loved ones, yet they are still peaceful people. The difference has to do with intentions. Cruel people experience some form of gratification when they inflict pain on others. They have developed a belief that if others are to learn or change, it will depend on them pushing others around, hurting them, or putting them in their place.

This is a fundamental error of thinking in the attempt to influence or change behavior in others. Get sufficient pain, penalty, or punishment, and you will surely be motivated! We all need to be held accountable for our actions, but the only thing punishment does is stop a behavior. It does little to teach a new one. The cruel person actually believes such things as:

- If I honk and scream at you, it surely will motivate you to drive differently in the future.
- If I demean you on the job, you will learn quicker.
- The rougher I am, the more you will tow the line.
- The more fear I inflict upon you, the more diligent you will become.

There is clear evidence in these situations that the only outcome we can count on for sure is the escalation of tension and increased conflict rather than de-escalation.

The *second* difference between the cruel and the kind is the perception of where the tension comes from. The cruel person believes that all his or her problems reside externally. This flawed thinking involves such thoughts as, "Others are most certainly responsible for my misery. I couldn't possibly have anything to do with the fact that I am hateful...angry...aggressive. She brings out the worst in me. He pushes me into a corner to make me act this way." In contrast, the peaceful person believes that there is a choice about how to act in a given set of circumstances.

The *third* difference between the cruel and the kind is empathy. Peaceful people know how others feel. Mean people only are capable of understanding their own feelings. Peaceful people are sensitive to other people's feelings and pain. The average normal-neurotic may find him- or herself in occasional cruel moods when he or she fails to have empathy.

The *fourth* major difference centers around our primitive instincts for attacking others. The cruel person has a string of simple prejudices based on jealousy. Along with the lack of empathy, when we are acting like a jerk, we seek reasons to believe that other people's differences are responsible for our pain. If left unchecked, average people can act like jerks, and their thoughts may sound like: "I am resentful of your opinion, happiness, emotional affluence, relationships, psychological possessions, and basic status of life. How dare you be happy while I am still miserable! How dare you flaunt your wellness! Stop enjoying life! This thing you have (that I don't) is what is keeping me from my own personal happiness. Your happiness persecutes and oppresses me. Therefore, if I mistreat you, I am justified in doing so."

These four major differences are not like an on-off or all-or-nothing condition. Each of us has varying degrees of these qualities. Some have better impulse control; some have a more sensitive conscience; others tend to do less blaming than most. In the end, however, we are all capable of being jerks at different times and in different situations. The hardcore jerk just happens to be more extreme more often.

Where is your jerk?

Before we examine the seven most common jerks, it is also important to ask yourself, "Where is your jerk?" We can be infected by jerks by merely reading about them, or we may have to work or live with them. Each type of jerk and his or her influence on your life may determine the amount of energy you have given them to have power over your life. Your jerk may be any of these:

- **Distant jerks** – These are the terrorists or the criminals we see in the news. Often there is very little actual face-to-face contact with them, but we feel as though our lives are tainted by their actions.

- **Everyday jerks** – These are the road ragers and the strangers who disrupt our daily living.

- **Neighboring jerks** – These are the people we live around or see in our social lives at Little League games, or PTA meetings, or community functions. We have to be around them even if we do not like it.

- **Workday jerks** – We have to communicate with them and perform daily tasks with them. Sometimes we spend more of our waking hours with them than with our loved ones and family, so we have to be careful because they have the potential to have enormous power over our day. They can take their toll on us but not necessarily have power over us.

- **Powerful jerks** – These are the jerks we have to answer to in our day-to-day responsibilities. They may be someone in charge of us on the job, or hold our mortgage or our contract, or have some financial power in our lives. These can be the most destructive because they can be devious and hold something over us just because they have the power to do so. They may hold our futures in their hands and can ruin some of our material comforts by keeping us fearful if we do not give in to their demands.

- **Close-to-your-heart jerks** – Yes, we may even live with them or be related to them. These relationships may be the longest-term associations in our lives. You can leave jobs, but some relatives never go away.

Many jerks may be in your life, and they may be capable of much damage. As you become a better Jerk Whisperer, you need to understand their motives and their behaviors. You also need to understand how much influence you have over your own life either to allow them to control you or not. Sometimes people relinquish a lot of power to someone who never directly affects them, and soon their stressors become products of their imagination.

The seven most common jerks
(and their baggage)

The seven most common jerks are the Mean, the Persecuted, the Self-Centered, the Entitled, the Competitive, the Ignorant, and the Crabby. They are placed in this order from the most dangerous to the least dangerous. Most Dangerous:

- Are most harmful to others
- Have a level of cruelty (lack of conscience)
- Have the highest level of pathology in the form of a personality disorder

Least Dangerous are individuals who:

- Are well-meaning
- Are unintentional in their behaviors
- Are more normal-neurotic in nature (rather than psychopathological)

Each of these jerks has patterns of behaving and thinking that I define by six questions.

First, what is their motto? The jerks' motto has to do with baggage or the fundamental role they see for themselves.

Second, where do they thrive? This is where they get their strength.

Third, what is their blindspot? The blindspot makes up the things they don't see in themselves but others do.

Fourth, What are the tools they use for hurting others?

Fifth, Why should we pity them?

Sixth, and most importantly, the Jerk Whisperer needs to believe in change and ask: Why they are worth changing? And why should we hold out hope for them?

> People in hell, where do they tell people to go?
> —*Red Skelton*

The Mean Jerk

When Brian began to struggle in his marriage, his wife moved out. They were never meant to be together. After spending a weekend away from home, he returned to his apartment, and every item in it had been ruined. Not a single item had been completely destroyed, but each item had been meticulously broken or altered just enough so that it was unusable. All of his suit coats had the back cut out of them, every pair of shoes had one hole drilled in them, his dress ties were cut in half, and the bottoms of drawers were smashed. A chip was taken out of each piece of glassware, a leg was missing from each piece of furniture, and every appliance had its internal mechanism broken, then put back together. The entire apartment looked neat upon first glance, but every item was ruined just enough so that it could not be repaired but had to be thrown away, right down to the kitchen clock that was taken apart and had the minute and hour hands removed, then put back together.

Brian had been the victim of a Mean Jerk. It was his father-in-law who always calmly inflicted pain on anyone who crossed him. In Brian's case, the man had spent at least two days ruining everything in the apartment. It would have taken less time to load the items into a moving van and steal them, but that was too easy; the jerk's goal was to make Brian feel pain with every ruined item he discovered in his home.

Casey was the athletic director at a small college. He was a father, a loyal employee, and he gave to his community. Over the years, he had minor disagreements with some employees, but overall, he was beloved by most of the students, faculty, and administration.

One day, a new employee claimed that Casey was unfair to her. Instead of working to remediate the problem she went to the local newspaper and made a claim of sexual harassment. She filed a lawsuit, and the landslide began. She systematically set out to destroy his reputation. The claim was enough to garner a lot of attention, including getting Casey's picture in the paper with a headline. Eventually, Casey was found innocent, but not before putting him and his family through hell. In the end, Casey's professional life was ruined. When the case was cleared, the paper did not even run an article to clear his name. The pain will be carried with him forever.

Mean Jerks are just plain cruel. Pain is their goal, objective, and intended outcome. They can do it in overt, rageful ways or in subtle, sneaky ways. Their intention is not just to get even, but to destroy and inflict a lot of pain. They are pathological, but in their minds, they need to do this to others, and they justify their cruelty by believing that lashing out is their strength.

Mean Jerks can also be sneaky, sneaky, sneaky. They are so insecure that they frequently avoid facing others or being direct. They do not believe in getting even; they believe in getting ahead of others on the pain meter. They want you to hurt more than they are hurting, and since they are always in pain, they also are always dishing it out.

Motto for life (baggage): I will smile when you writhe more than I do.

The value of my life is in direct proportion to the amount of pain I can bring to others. What is a little rough treatment? If you are too weak for life, it is your fault. Mess with me, and you will go down with as much pain as possible and for as long as possible.

Favorite place to be (where they thrive): Anywhere there are vulnerable people, and anytime they can create an excuse to dish out pain.

Something you never hear them say (blind spot): I regret mistreating people in my life.

The tools for hurting others/Why they suck the life out of us (habits – what they are doing that irritates us most): Mean Jerks are on a constant quest to discover every person's Achilles heel. They want to find the thing that hurts most and use it to do that very thing.

Struggles (why we should pity them): There is a missing link in their brain, and mostly it has to do with a lack of empathy. They go through life gritting their teeth. Mean Jerks have less of a conscience than any other kind of jerk. It is as though they are wired differently.

Why they are worth changing (the hope we hold for them): If they ever "get it," they can help to heal the lives they have ruined. Sometimes mean jerks burn out and can see the pain they have caused. When they have this revelation, they may even make healing others a life quest. It's like the gang leader who comes back to the old neighborhood and becomes a counselor for wayward youth. Or the Scrooge who is shaken so badly that he turns his life toward generosity.

When I hear somebody sigh, "Life is hard," I am always tempted to ask, "Compared to what?"

—*Sydney J. Harris*

The Persecuted Jerk

Wendell got passed over for his raise. The management indicated to him that he had not met the criteria to be promoted.

To Wendell, however, it is crystal clear. It was because he is white, and male, and catholic. Yes, life is inherently unfair to him because he is thin, and Republican, and he did not get his degree from an Ivy League university, and he is too tall, and Irish, and has freckles, and is lactose intolerant, and has a New Jersey accent, and once supported the Red Sox baseball team, and has blue eyes, and drives an import car. Yes, these are only a few of the reasons why he got passed over for the job. He will never make as much money as he could because he is left-handed, and a vegetarian, and his hair is thinning. Life will always be an uphill battle because he does not get fair treatment because he has an overactive thyroid, and he believes in realism, and he has a trick wrist that does not enable him to type as fast as everyone else (society never makes the proper accommodations for people with trick wrists), and he has a non-mainstream computer, but since everyone else in the office uses a mainstream computer, it means that most of his work has to have special accommodations.

When Wendell enters a room, everyone moves away emotionally. "It's because they are a bunch of racists, sexists, idiots…. If only they were as insightful and brilliant as I am. It's really hard to be me. Even when I shuffle the cards for solitaire, they try to stack up against me. If only you knew how hard it is to be me!"

Motto for life (baggage): It's your fault that the world is in a mess. It's your fault that my life is a mess. If I had your privileges, I would have everything, including your happiness. Therefore, I have every right to mistreat you, talk about you, find fault in you, and try to convince others to hate you too! Everyone is prejudiced except me!

Favorite place to be (where they thrive): Persecuted Jerks spend an extraordinary amount of time in the Library of the Victimized, finding more books titled *Why I Am Mistreated.* They also hang out anywhere they can find their fellow miserable crusaders. If they could not complain and if they did not have loathing for others, they would not have anything to say at all. Intelligent Persecuted Jerks may seek safe ivory towers to preach from but never get their hands dirty by trying to do something about their causes.

Something you never hear them say (blindspot): I guess life wasn't as bad as I thought it was. Perhaps I've personalized things I shouldn't have. Sure I've had some tough breaks, but I will put all those lessons to good work and make the world a better place.

The tools for hurting others/Why they suck the life out of us (habits – what they are doing that irritates us most): Persecuted Jerks can be the constant moaners, but they also can be martyrs, using logic and persuasion to lure others into their world of misery. (They've already used a ton of logic to convince themselves of why their misery is justified.) Persecuted Jerks may sometimes appear to be crusaders for life's injustices because it is their only topic of conversation. They often are separated from other people because they are the whiners and never the doers. They complain about injustices but rarely step up to address the causes. They believe that an activist is a person who complains the loudest. You may find them in the extreme overt hate groups (racists, sexists), or they may try to portray themselves as human rights activists as an excuse to hate: "All people of (fill in the blank of their particular group) are evil!"

Struggles (why we should pity them): They were probably mistreated somewhere along the way and lacked the tools to bounce back. They spend their lives convincing others how they have been victimized. They fail to take risks to be happy because misery is predictable. One of their constant struggles is the belief that everyone is abandoning them.

Why they are worth changing (the hope we hold for them): They still have energy; it is simply misguided. Persecuted Jerks are classic victimists (instead of scientists). They are interested in information that supports their oppression-related misery. If they were interested in placing their energy in a positive journey, they could collect data to help others and be a true force in the fight against oppression. All they need is a revelation to see the beauty and potential in the world. Persecuted Jerks have learned to see themselves as miserable crusaders. Our hope for them is that they can become happy crusaders. The major obstacle is not being able to take responsibility for miserable thoughts. They have a hard time with hope because it is riskier than pessimism.

> Talent is God-given; be humble.
> Fame is man-given; be thankful.
> Conceit is self-given; be careful.
>
> *—John Wooden*

The Self-Centered Jerk

"... and then I tried to help, then I fixed it, and if it wasn't for me, this place would still be a mess. Thank God for me. I am pretty darn important..." said John. After speaking for eighty of the ninety minutes in the meeting, he concluded, "Well, thanks for your input. We really got a lot done today."

The rest of the people at the meeting sat in silence. Each one of them had been burned by John. John is the center of the universe. He is special, charismatic, important, needed, infallible, and for the most part just plain perfect in a world of imperfect lesser people. The only time he listens to others is if they are stroking his ego or if you are giving him information that he later can use against you.

♦ ♦ ♦

Heather sat in silence. Her sister Kate had just finished telling her that she had been insensitive. "You didn't need to snap at those people at the dinner party; they are friends of mine. You were very rude to them."

Heather paused, then lashed out. "Oh, I suppose I just don't have the right to be passionate about anything, do I? When I simply have an opinion, I'm rude? Well, thanks. I guess you are just one more person who wants to tell me to grow up! Well, I've got news for you. We're done. We're not talking anymore. You're dead to me!"

You can fake nice, but you cannot fake good. You are either a good person who is guided by good intentions or you are not.

Self-Centered Jerks are egocentric. Their narcissism allows them to become heavily involved in facades and false personas. They will be anything to anyone if it will result in the chance that the other person will return some praise. But any time praise is lacking, they are certain it is an indicator of antagonism.

To some degree, Self-Centered Jerks are antisocial because they lack a conscience, but they are not as devious as Cruel Jerks; they are simply oblivious to others' opinions. As aging progresses, they struggle with the changes. Since they are accustomed to psychological and physical personas, they see wrinkles and gray hair as the enemy. They often see change and disagreements as disloyalty and personal abandonment.

Motto for life (baggage): Everyone has problems; it is just that mine are more important than anyone else's. Bad stuff seems to happen more often to me, but I just do not understand it—how could life be so rough on someone as beautiful as me? If it were not for me, this place would be a real mess. I cannot understand why anyone would not praise me.

Favorite place to be (where they thrive): In front of a mirror or on a stage. If one is not available, they will seek out others who can stroke their ego.

Something you never hear them say (blindspot): Tell me about your life! And I'll listen without the need to tell you about my life!

The tools for hurting others/Why they suck the life out of us (habits – what they are doing that irritates us most): Self-Centered Jerks only help those who suck up to them. They can be charming but also trustbandits. They use their charm to gather information from you and then may use it against you. In the end, if you are not a sycophant, you are viewed as disloyal. These jerks also see themselves as trustworthy. They love to gossip, disparage others, and use gossipy information to elevate their status (in other's minds, as well as their own).

Struggles (why we should pity them): They are constantly disillusioned as to why the world does not respond to them in ways they think it should. It takes a lot of energy to be self-centered. They also believe they have the right to interrupt, talk over, raise their voice, and be in complete control of any conversation. But do not dare interrupt them! If you do, you are rude! Self-Centered Jerks' unfortunate doom is that they cannot see their own rudeness, but those around them can.

Why they are worth changing (the hope we hold for them): It may take the Self-Centered Jerk a mid-life crisis to understand that they are like everyone else. Developmentally, they are stuck. They are like the two-year-old who stares out the window of the car and says, "Look, Mommy! The moon is following me!" Underneath it all, they are loaded with sensitivity; it is just that they cannot get past the idea that other people may have views, perspectives, opinions, and feelings as valid as their own.

> You never appreciate your language until you go to a foreign country that doesn't have the courtesy to speak English.
>
> —*Steve Martin*

The Entitled Jerk

Stan shook his head. "These people," he muttered under his breath. "It just makes me so mad." He was angry as he counted the items in the basket of the customer standing in line in front of him. Soon it was more than he could stand. He had had enough. It was time to speak up. "Excuse me, Ma'am! I believe you have fourteen items in your basket. This is a ten-item-or-less line." He placed his hands on his hips and glared at the woman.

Jill gripped the wheel of her car as she steered through the parking lot. Finally she slammed on her brakes. She was incensed that this was the third day in a row that she had arrived at the employee lot and had not found a parking place. However, her mood shifted to excitement as she spotted a parking place, only to endure heartbreak when she drove up close enough to see that the place was taken up by a motorcycle. She pulled out a pen and paper. It was time to leave a note. "Dear Idiot, Day after day I see your stupid little motorcycle taking up an entire spot where a car could be parked...."

Judy politely smiled at the clerk. "My oh my! I forgot to get lettuce. Do you mind?" She ran out of the line and then returned four minutes later. As she got back in the line, she turned and apologized to the six people who were waiting behind her. "I'm sorry to keep all of you waiting, I'm sorry. I'm sorry. I'm sorry to keep all of you waiting. Thank you so much for your patience."

Motto for life (baggage): Everyone has rights. It just so happens that I have more than everyone else. I own this lane on the highway, this spot in your restaurant, this space in the grocery store, and if you invade my space, my time, my world, if you inconvenience me in any way, ye shall endure my wrath.

Favorite place to be (where they thrive): In any movie theater with a cellphone in hand.

Something you never hear them say (blindspot): Gosh, I'm so sorry, after reflecting on my behavior. I realize I was rude! Gosh, I'm sorry. Did I offend you? I was insensitive.

The tools for hurting others/Why they suck the life out of us (habits – what they are doing that irritates us most): Entitled Jerks spend most of their life getting even with the world. Note: They are the only ones who are entitled to talk during movies, pass notes at meetings, use sarcasm whenever and wherever possible, and clog up lanes on the highway. Quite simply, they are special. "Everyone is an idiot except me!" For most of us, when we apologize, we try to change our behavior the next time around. In the case of Entitled Jerks, their apologies are really lies; they are merely apologizing to clear their own guilt, not to get it right.

Struggles (why we should pity them): Clearly Entitled Jerks are among some of the most ignorant people on the planet. The ignorance is not necessarily malicious; it is simply a conscious effort to ignore facts, truths, and common sense. Somewhere along the way, these jerks were told that life is filled with people who are inferior to them. The role models in their life taught them that life centers around them.

Why they are worth changing (the hope we hold for them): If the light ever goes on in their heads, it will be a revelation, and Entitled Jerks will have tremendous insight into human abuses. The shame they will feel will be a great motivator.

> The contented man is never poor.
> The discontented man is never rich.
>
> —*Bob Phillips*

The Competitive Jerk

"It looks like someone's lawn is not as thick as some other lawns again this year!" shouted Jack. Each year he threw out a few barbs to his neighbor in regard to the appearance of his lawn. And shrubs, and Christmas decorations, and the wax job on the car, and his kids' Little League trophies, and raises he earned, and anything else he could possibly use as a comparison.

"Oh, it was horrible. When my daughter started to break out with the measles, she…" Jen was cut off in mid-sentence by a voice that came from behind her. "Try having three kids with the measles at the same time!" shouted Wanda. On her job, she was known as "Wanda-one-upper." Whenever anyone in the office shared experiences of their children, or vacations, or assorted trials in life, Wanda had a story to top it.

Wanda and Jack are insecure jerks who constantly need to tell others that they have had to endure more, or that they have done more, been more places, worked harder, had more fun, and laughed more than anyone else. The key is "more." They cannot stand it if they cannot be the captain of the team. They need to convince themselves that whatever endeavor is out there in life, they have exceeded everyone else's. These two Competitive Jerks are the same because they always have to win. Wanda needs to win the story; Jack needs to win at everything that is going on now.

Competitive Jerks need to compete at everything. You could be shopping for wreaths for a funeral, and the Competitive Jerk will buy a bigger one and tell you he is grieving more than anyone else. If they ever irritate others, they hide behind the line: "Hey if you can't take a joke…."

Competitive Jerks are always looking for comparative data. If they get ahead in a game, they like to punish, rub it in, howl and squeal, even when they beat someone at throwing crumpled papers into a wastebasket. They are especially adept at positioning on the highway—"I'll get there ahead of that guy"—as they dart in and out of traffic, pick the fastest line in the supermarket, and keep glancing into the garage stalls to see if their car gets the oil change faster than the guy who brought his car in at the same time. For Competitive Jerks, there is a finish line everywhere in life. If they finish second, they are always ready to scream "Foul!"

Motto for life (baggage): I cannot help it. I am just a winner at heart! I am sorry, I just have to be first at everything! Come on, quit your whining. You just cannot stand it when I win at everything!

Favorite place to be (where they thrive): In the bookstore searching for social steroids by finding books such as *How to Justify Your Road Rage! Stay More Alert to All Those People Who Are Idiots! Why You Have the Right to Be a Jackass! Sharpen Your Attack Skills!* and *How to Never Lose a Battle—Ever!*

Something you never hear them say (blindspot): I don't need to have the last word on everything! I'm sorry. Let me step out of the way. Please, you go first.

The tools for hurting others/Why they suck the life out of us (habits – what they are doing that irritates us most): "Come on, it's just a friendly game of office darts." They have an edge to them that can be deceiving.

Struggles (why we should pity them): Chances are, Competitive Jerks learned long ago that the only way to happiness is to win at everything. There is nothing wrong with a need to prosper and excel at life's endeavors. A competitive edge can be the source of spirit and drive. The only problem is that these jerks have no concern for anyone else's welfare in the process. When they understand that they can compete and still be compassionate, they can develop the potential to be great leaders.

Why they are worth changing (the hope we hold for them): Competitive Jerks often will harbor a great memory of all of their defeats and conquests. They keep a ledger on who they believe hurt them and those who were on their team. When they outgrow the need to win and work toward *us* winning, they will find peace in their lives and be the best teammate in a group effort.

Know yourself. Don't accept your dog's admiration as conclusive evidence that you are wonderful.

—*Ann Landers*

The Ignorant Jerk

Kenneth came to every meeting looking for something wrong in everyone else's view. He was able to cite at least one example to confirm why it would not work: "It is a bad idea; I have seen it tried before; I have been there; there was a statistic on that...." Whenever Kenneth did not attend the meetings, his colleagues got a lot done and enjoyed discourse on important issues.

Kathy stomped into the school with an agenda. She was hell-bent on meeting with the principal and reading her the riot act on how this school should be run. She was there to defend her child who was sent home for bullying. She cited an article that said that children need to learn to be tough to deal with the bullies, and the real problem is the whiney child who always complains about the bullies.

Kenneth and Kathy are the types of people who need to be right about everything and always find an example on which to argue. Once they get into their battle, they never back down. Ignorant Jerks have fragile egos, and it is difficult for them to consider anyone's view but their own. You will hear them say things like: "Hey, I was spanked, and I turned out okay. Hey, I once bought a station wagon, and it fell apart—all station wagons are garbage. I went to Paris and was treated badly—all people from Paris are rotten. We've never deviated from that policy—if we change now, things will surely fall apart."

Often, Ignorant Jerks are so insecure that they stretch truths and facts, or they may even create statistics for the sole purpose of being right. They are not just experts; they are experts on everything.

Motto for life (baggage): I am the most insightful, intelligent person on earth. I am always right. In fact, I am rightfully and righteously righter than anyone I have ever met.

Favorite place to be (where they thrive): Online, they can find an answer for everything (and everyone knows that everything on the Internet is true).

Something you never hear them say (blindspot): Hmmm… let me stop and think about your viewpoint. There is a chance I could have missed something, or I could be wrong.

The tools for hurting others/Why they suck the life out of us (habits – what they are doing that irritates us most): Ignorant Jerks are harvesters of the shallow and inaccurate. They will fight to the end rather than see another view. They can be extremely irritating by giving advice to parents (even if they have never had children), giving advice on finances (even though they have run up $30,000 on their credit cards), giving advice on health (as they cough, wheeze, and order more french fries), and telling everyone at the gym how to be more fit (as they attempt a push-up).

Struggles (why we should pity them): Ignorant Jerks are lonely, disconnected individuals. They are afraid that if they begin to see another's viewpoint, it will make them vulnerable, average, and unable to be superior. They also have an incredible inferiority complex. They probably grew up around a person who was always right, and in defense, they looked for every opportunity to be right about something.

Why they are worth changing (the hope we hold for them): The sad lonely shells that Ignorant Jerks carry around have become sources of misery. Their level of naivety needs an "aha" experience in which they see how they could connect with others and not be so lonely if they only let their guard down for a minute to realize that it is okay to be normal and not know everything. They have not yet learned that the smartest people on the planet are those who are astutely aware of how little they know.

> You let go of grief when you save another person's life. You let go of anger by easing another person's anger.
>
> —*African Proverb*

The Crabby Jerk

"I get this way when I get crabby," said Lona. She had spent the morning snapping at every person in the office. "You should know better and stay out of my way when I'm having one of these days."

"You kids shut up back there! Have some respect!" Andrew crumpled the map and threw it on his wife's lap. The kids sat like statues in the back seat. Dad is in one of his "driving" moods, and we are lost again.

"Bear with me! I get this way when the orders get stacked up!" screamed Chad. Everyone in the restaurant hustled around in order to not push Manager Chad's buttons.

Lona, Andrew, and Chad are the most common jerks. There is a little bit of the Crabby Jerk in every human on earth. These may be good, well-meaning individuals, but they lash out depending on the stress or moods they are experiencing that day. They may be tired, cranky, and edgy, and they often take it out on loved ones. Occasionally, they may expect everyone else to figure out their moods, and they justify their rough treatment as some force outside of their control.

Motto for life (baggage): I can't help it! It's just the way I feel!

Favorite place to be (where they thrive): Crabby Jerks just want to get away; sometimes they just want to crawl out of their own skin. When they get crabby, they do not like themselves. Whenever things are not going their way, they know they need to be alone to diffuse their bombs, and time alone may mean that they will have to realize it was their behavior, not the behavior of others, escalating the tension.

Something you never hear them say (blindspot): I just need to stop and take a deep breath.

The tools for hurting others/Why they suck the life out of us (habits – what they are doing that irritates us most): In the moment, Crabby Jerks have a justification for every action and may expect others to be mind-readers. "You should know I'm having a bad day! You should know better!"

Struggles (why we should pity them): Often, the Crabby Jerk is just a normal person, with normal-neurotic episodes, and it can happen to any of us. Crabby Jerks are people with enormous pride, and their biggest stumbling block is that they are unable to drop their shield and ask for emotional support. In the moment that they are crabby, they have misplaced priorities, as they place the value of a task ahead of the value of a relationship.

Why they are worth changing (the hope we hold for them): The anger and the fussiness are just masks for justifying Crabby Jerks' moods. They may be well-meaning and wonderful people who are struggling to be better. Their problem is that in their moment of fussiness, they are extending blame to something outside of themselves rather than inside themselves. When they reflect, they can have great potential for change. They may be overextended and need to slow down to reduce these episodes. If they do slow down, they can develop gratefulness for those around them instead of resentment. The redeeming quality that Crabby Jerks have is that they are always working on themselves. They know they need to reduce the number of crabby episodes. They are never afraid to apologize, and they know they are not perfect.

Admit it.

We are all capable of acting like a jerk.

There are times when even the nicest and kindest people among us are capable of acting like a jerk. We are all guilty of being short-tempered with a loved one, reacting a little more than we should, or just having a crabby day. The good news is this: You can give yourself a break because you are human. The key is to engage in a lifelong mission to be reflective and try to reduce your moments of lashing out at others. Maybe you've felt entitled, self-persecuted, competitive, or just plain crabby. As long as you can see it in the mirror, you can change it. You can develop these skills and make the world a better place. All jerks are worth changing, and you are too.

Step Six:

Practicing the Ten Essential Skills of the Jerk Whisperer

We often allow the jerks of the world to consume our thoughts, and when we do this, they have conquered us. The most dangerous weapon they possess is not a club, a gun, or a knife. The most dangerous item of their destruction is not found in their words or their deeds. The most dangerous thing they possess is the corner of our mind which they occupy. If for only one moment they have upset our genuineness or dented our authenticity, they have done exactly what they set out to do—cause damage.

If we can create a new set of skills in our quest to find peace in this world, we can become the opposite of the damage seekers. We can transform ourselves into ambassadors of reparation. We can become diplomats for civility and become part of the revolution for change we so desperately need in this world. Earlier in the book, I shared a quote from Eric Hoffer, who said, "Rudeness is the weak man's imitation of strength." There are many imitations of strength, and we have to find within ourselves the psychological will to persevere. It takes a lot more strength to be kind than it does to be mean.

> Many people lose their tempers merely from seeing you keep yours.
>
> *—Frank Moore Colby*

Skill #1
A Jerk Whisperer practices not reacting

During the course of a day, most of us will witness an exchange between people that we may deem improper or rude. We see someone's inappropriate rudeness, and we think that is wrong. We also occasionally catch ourselves doing something or treating someone in a manner that we believe is contrary to our character. But do we think about how we can practice unlearning these habits?

Maybe the most important lessons in life are those in which we unlearn habits, as opposed to learning them. Dropping old habits can set us free. The things that we let go of often result in more growth than the things to which we cling. A fundamental skill of an effective Jerk Whisperer is the ability to avoid reacting to tension, rudeness, or hostility. In other words, when stressors strike, we need to ask ourselves: "Is it possible for me to be peaceful without the need to go into a defensive, offensive, or attack mode?"

Most of the time when we overreact, it is not a life or death situation. An incompetent clerk does not deserve our wrath. A distracted driver does not deserve a deathmatch in the Roman Coliseum. Most of the world does not deserve the hostility it has to endure. In order to create change, we need to practice something as simple as not reacting.

One-minute reflection:

1. Old habits can be dropped in simple ways, starting with some of the minor stress factors. Do you start your day with a series of discontented moments based on traffic or the dishes in the sink? Practice physically letting go. Start by asking yourself, "Where is my stress?" Unclench your jaw, relax your fists, and try to stand still for just three seconds (that is all it really takes).

2. Take moments out of your day to catch yourself, take a deep breath, and practice not reacting. As you review your typical reactions to life's chaos, you need to be aware of the evidence of self-induced stress. For example, do you find yourself letting out big sighs while you stand in line, or complaining about the car in front of you, or shaking your head every time a clerk is slower than you would like him to be? These are not crisis situations, but you have made them into just that. Practice calmness. Practice a readiness for calmness. Before you know it, you will be handling real crises with efficiency and letting more of the minor stressors wash over you.

There is plenty of time in life to be in a crisis. Do not create one.

> Choose to be a love-finder rather than a fault-finder.
>
> *—Gerald Jampolsky*

Skill #2

A Jerk Whisperer treats every relationship as though he will need help from that person for many years into the future

We know from decades of research that we can change our lives by changing the way we think. Our thoughts can actually alter the chemistry of the brain. Research suggests that we are capable of altering our moods, decision-making capabilities, and relational skills by merely starting (and ending) the day with positive thoughts, words, or music. This small change at the day's dawn can affect everything we do during our waking hours.

The same holds true with regard to relationships. If we start every relationship by recognizing the good in others before we focus on what annoys us, we tend to treat others more positively.

If we do not like the way we act or react in certain situations, it may be that we simply have the wrong mindset for that day. The skill to *treat every relationship as though you will need help from that person for many years* begins its journey by seeing the best in others and seeing the best in the world around us. We live in a throwaway culture, and we tend to view our connections to many things as a temporary emotionless endeavor. Unfortunately, this bleeds into our relationships. We often treat people as though they are only a temporary engagement with no real reason for an emotional investment. If you have ever been treated like an object without a soul, you know how this feels. If you have ever been treated as though you were disposable, you know how this feels.

The evidence of an honorable person is also found in how he or she treats the physical world, and it sets the plate for how we treat people. To respect all of life's creations is one of the greatest virtues we may acquire. Ichiro Suzuki is one of the greatest baseball players in the history of major league baseball, and he has remarkable self-control. In an interview, he was asked why he never threw a tantrum or threw down a bat or glove while he played. He said that his behavior was a reflection of his respect for the maker of the bat, the ball, and the glove. He said that some person somewhere had crafted the piece of wood with his hands, and to disrespect the bat was to disrespect the honor of the person who took pride in the creation. He simply indicated that it was not his place in this world to dishonor that person's work.

That interview with Ichiro has always inspired me. He demonstrated reverence for the connection between one's personal nobility and the dignity of the greater world. In the end, respect is one of the greatest virtues we can build in ourselves and in others. If we can extend it past humans and into all objects, we can bring even greater homage to all living things.

If you have ever worked around a person who supervises others but who never says anything positive about them, the supervisees know how it can take a toll on their well-being and the entire atmosphere in which they live. After a while, apathy sets in, and cynicism follows. All of us have to live around these people, and to be an effective Jerk Whisperer, you have to decide whether you will allow these instances to be your lesson instead of your personal torture device.

When we turn these instances into a lesson, we realize how we can improve another's frame of mind, productivity, and sense of self-worth. On the other hand, if at any point in our lives we say, "I don't need this person anymore," we discard the relationship. It is rather like the person who saves everything he believes to be of value. If you see the good in people and things, you will nurture their potential.

It is important to acknowledge everyone (especially those in our daily circle of people), and in doing so, acknowledge that they all have value and importance in this world. If we see people as objects—"Get busy…. I need this done…. You need to get on this…"—eventually they will come to understand how we disvalue them, and in that case, it indicates that they have only utility value and not human value.

On the other hand, when we enter the workplace and see a person who is real, a person who breathes, feels, has friends, loved ones, children, and a real life, we tend to treat him or her with a level of humane decency. The person who sees others as objects ultimately will do more damage in this world than good.

I enjoy saying, "Hi!" to many people I pass in the day (unless they totally creep me out). On campus, I will nod and greet faculty, administrators, students, and staff. In public, I will do the same to clerks, waitresses, or whomever else is around me.

Several years ago, a student said, "Dr. Birchak, I saw you in the store this weekend."

I asked, "Why didn't you say hi?"

"I didn't want to bother you, but when I saw you, it seemed like you were having such a good day. You were standing in a line in a grocery store, and you were chatting with the clerk and laughing. I thought, wow, he enjoys life in all kinds of situations and not just in our college courses!"

I kept wondering what she must have been thinking. It was as though in her mind, I leave the college every day and become a grump! She then went on to say, "It actually made my day. I was whining and feeling sorry for myself, and I saw you and realized, as you said in class, that we can be happy in most situations in life. I then changed my attitude and had a great day!"

I love the quote above from Gerald Jampolsky when he says, "Choose to be a love-finder rather than a fault-finder." It is along the line of the "glass half-full" outlook, but it is much more than that. If you constantly look for the good in others, you will never discard a relationship.

At any given point in our life, when we decide to go on a tirade, tell off somebody, permanently discard a relationship, or verbally cast aside another human being, we have altered our potential. We have lost a little bit of our self-respect, our integrity, our significance, and our promise in this world.

If you treat every relationship as though you will need to collaborate and bond with that person for the next twenty years, you will never burn a bridge in your life. This is not only a philosophy; it is a virtue and a daily habit to see others as real humans, not just as objects that you have in your life for getting your needs met. Every discarded relationship results in the devaluing of your existence and the devaluing of your world.

We need each other for the remainder of our lives and beyond. (Your children need a kinder world, too.)

One-minute reflection:

Make up your mind that tomorrow you will identify at least one person with whom you will interact differently. He or she may simply be doing his or her job with you or for you. Make a conscious decision to see him or her and validate him or her at least enough so that he or she may feel that his or her life has relevance. It will take you less than ten seconds, but it may make his or her day. Every secretary, custodian, clerk, waitress, and co-worker, deserves to be treated with dignity and respect. These are living, breathing, loving, caring, compassionate people who deserve more than my nod to sack my groceries, send out my letters, answer my phone, wait on my table, or empty my wastebasket. These are people who work and want the same things everyone wants. All of us want a decent life, a bit of gratitude, and a pair of open arms at the end of the day. Why not give them these things at work, too? (Although you may not want to hug everyone. It scares some people—but you know what I mean. Hug them with your words and validate them).

Opinions which justify cruelty are inspired by cruel impulses.

—*Bertrand Russell*

Skill #3
A Jerk Whisperer vents but does not disparage others

My wonderful wife Annie has dedicated her life to education. She is now an administrator, but at one time, she had one of the most difficult jobs in education. She worked with severely emotionally disturbed children in special education. At the end of a long day, she would come through the door, and the first thing I would ask her was, "How was your day?" I always let her go first because when she finished describing how her students acted that day, I had very little to say. If I tried to top her stories, I would have sounded pretty ridiculous. "Yeah, I had a tough day too…. My graduate students…um…yeah, they tried to bite and kick me too…." I knew what kind of a day she'd had, and she deserved to vent a little. We all deserve to vent; it is fairly natural. We need to verbalize the things in life that frustrate us.

Everyone needs to vent, but none of us will ever make positive changes in our lives during the times when we are speaking negatively of others. Whenever we are degrading people, spouting our hatred, tearing down others, going on long rants about the things we dislike in others, or saying mean things about others, we are revealing our character. When we take a moment to think about the people who are most annoying in this world, they are often the ones most guilty of disrespecting others. Whenever they are frustrated with life, they try to elevate themselves with unkind words about other people. Soon they have filled their minds with obsessions about their misery, and they cannot think of anything but blaming the people they have criticized.

Whenever my wife vented about her day, I never heard her say a bad word about anyone. She spoke of frustrations, but never spoke ill of the children she worked with. (In fact, the most troubled ones usually got more hugs—they needed it.) She never speaks ill of other faculty or administrators. She never has to think about it. It is a habit in her thinking and in her behavior. Unknowingly, she is demonstrating her character. The result is obvious in the fact that no one (and I emphasize *no one*) has ever said a bad word about her. People feel comfortable around her; people feel safe around her; people love her, and it is all because they know she does not see bad things in people; she sees the good. (I still have no idea what she sees in me, but I do believe I must be the luckiest guy on earth.)

There's no quicker way to develop a negative attitude than to disrespect others and spend time around people who do the same. If we avoid these people, we find that we enjoy life more; we look for the positive outcomes, and we seek out the positive people. There is a fundamental difference between venting and disrespecting. When a person vents, he is not complaining about other people; he is talking about the problem in "me." When a person speaks negatively of others, he is deflecting all of his problems onto "you." When we vent, we are trying to solve a problem in ourselves rather than blame it on others. When we disparage others, we are trying to persuade others to join us in our misery and our blame.

One-minute reflection:

1. When you reflect on your day today, examine who you believe is responsible for your misery. Do your thoughts immediately go to people you demonized? "That stupid co-worker! My idiot boss!" Try to turn that inward and reflect on your role in how you see those people and how you react to them. When you feel like saying bad things, stop and think about how you can rephrase it so that you take more responsibility.

2. Also examine how others react to you. What is the outward evidence that you are a disparager? What happens when a disparager enters a room? What happens when loving people enter a room? When you enter a room, what do people do? Their reaction to you will tell you what kind of person you are. Do they light up? "Hey, here comes Betty!" Or "Oh my goodness! Run for cover! Here comes Phil!"

3. Practice healthy venting (instead of unhealthy disparaging). Venting may even have healthy qualities because we are sorting things out, setting goals, and bringing or-

der to the chaos. We know we have to keep it to a minimum; otherwise, it becomes the color of paint by which we cover the entire world. Venting allows us to stick to the issue of what is frustrating us and how we can try to solve it. Disparaging others is an ego-driven exercise that solves nothing, demonstrates signs of a weak ego, and only fuels our misery. Every time we judge and speak disparagingly of others, we lose a little of our personal power because we are deflecting our personal responsibility for our attitude. We are saying, "It's your fault I'm miserable and hateful! You made me this way! I've become powerless to you!"

It is easier to be critical than to be right.
—*Benjamin Disraeli*

Skill #4
A Jerk Whisperer minimizes blame and maximizes validation

An effective Jerk Whisperer states everything non-blamefully but accepts the blame if responsible. This is a simple but very effective tool for communicating. All of us have to communicate our frustrations and our problems with others. Learning how to state problems non-blamefully removes the attack from our conversation. It may be as simple as removing the word "you" when we need to give feedback. "I am so angry when you leave the dishes in the sink!...when you don't pick up your socks...when you don't get your work done on time." Make your statements non-blamefully, and you will remove the finger pointing and the accusatory tone. "When I see the dishes in the sink.... When I see the socks on the floor... When I see unfinished work...."

If you can practice this daily, you will find less stress, tension, and emotion surrounding your issues. By removing blame, you open the door to conversing with civility.

Minimizing blame is actually a philosophical stance derived from existentialism. Accept the blame when you are responsible. This also opens doors because you can show that you are human. My father was an existential philosopher, but I didn't know it when I was young. I discovered it many years later when I was in my doctoral program. He only had an eighth grade education and worked in a factory most of his life, but he lived by the existential doctrine of choices and responsibility. If you did something stupid, you had to take responsibility for that action and not blame others.

My father raised his children with the "You had it coming" philosophy. I grew up without safety caps, safety helmets, and plugs to put over outlets. You were warned once, and whatever consequences occurred, you had to take responsibility for them.

When I was in the second grade, my brother (a short-statured fourth grader) and I were playing a cat and mouse game with a sixth grader. I threw a rock at the sixth grader, darted into the street, and consequently was struck by a car.* After the chaos of my brother running home to tell my parents—"Stevie got run over by a car!"—followed by the ambulance, hospital, needles, and stitches, I remember my mother standing over me trying to comfort me. I also remember the words of my existential philosopher father: "Well, you had it coming." These were the same words I'd heard when I ran my bicycle into a car,* when we put a huge firecracker under a tin can and the shrapnel tore the flesh on my arm* (another lovely hospital trip), when I broke a couple of teeth,* and when I was electrocuted by sticking things into a wall socket.* Each instance resulted in the

---

* Research suggests that children with attention deficit disorders tend to visit hospital emergency rooms with greater frequency than the general population. For the record, I took care of the average for the entire neighborhood.

philosopher's words, "Well, you had it coming." Each time, I was reminded that I am responsible for my life.

I think the thing that amazed me the most was also my father's uncanny ability to foretell the future accurately after these events. My father would say, "Well, you had it coming," followed by, "Betcha never do that again." He was very, very accurate. For the record, I have never again been hit by a car, or been blown up by a firecracker, or electrocuted since then (I knocked a few more teeth out, so he was not completely accurate, but who is perfect?)

The most important principle is this: if we accept blame for our mistakes (stupidity), we set ourselves up to learn. If we do not accept blame, we learn nothing. Most of what happens to us is our own responsibility. When we reflect on what we can do differently next time, we are learning. When we acquire a new habit (like not darting into the street, nor putting firecrackers under tin cans), we are acquiring wisdom.

As I grew up, I tried to question my father's perfect philosophy by asking about situations in which people had no control. I asked my dad, "How about that guy who got struck by lightning? Did he have it coming?" My father had that figured out too: "No, that was an act of God."

His life was simple, for about 99% of what happens in life, you had it coming; for the other 1%, it was an act of God. To this day, I carry that philosophy, and I do very little blaming. If I make a stupid financial decision, I had it coming. If I escalate tension in a relationship, I had it coming. I also encourage others to do the same. For instance, when a graduate student wants to argue a grade, I simply point out the errors and illustrate how he or she, "had it coming." I generally frame it a little nicer than that, but the message is simple: take responsibility.

On one occasion, I had a student go into great detail about how he did not deserve a grade that he had been given. On this occasion, I did not have my grade book with my grading criteria, so I said what any self-respecting professor would say in that situation: "Your grade? It was an act of God." (Truthfully, I must admit that I've never done this, but I'm ready in case I ever have the opportunity someday.)

The bottom line is this: if we fail to see our behavior as something we can control, we no longer are able to make it better. Think of adults and kids today, whose only response is, "It's not my fault. He made me angry. She made me miserable. He made me lash out." They have lost their ability to be the authors of their own lives. Henry Ward Beecher summed up his sentiments about responsibility and excuses well when he said, "Hold yourself responsible for a higher standard than anyone else expects of you. Never excuse yourself."

When we minimize blame, we also need to maximize the validation of others. As social creatures, one of the most horrible feelings we ever experience is when we feel we do not matter. In social psychology research, there are numerous examples of humans driven to despair when they believe that their life does not count. In the military, "shunning" was banned as punishment because of its devastating psychological effects. In adolescence, teens are driven to suicide as a result of being tortured by the "in crowd." In the workplace, there is no quicker way to drive someone to anger, depression, and revenge than to make that person believe that he or she is irrelevant.

All humans have an innate drive to feel relevant. When you are around people who sincerely recognize and validate your efforts, you begin to form the belief that your life is meaningful. In contrast, the effects can be devastating when cruel people withhold this recognition as a way to inflict pain. You know this feeling if you have ever worked on a job and you have said to yourself, "Wow, I've worked here for six months, and I have never heard one good thing about my work; I'm only told when I make mistakes!"

This is a great lesson for Jerk Whisperers. We have to vow to ourselves never to make anyone feel that low. Validating others is second nature for peaceful, influential people because they keep their eyes open and offer genuine appreciation every time it is due. It can be as simple as telling someone you appreciate her time or recognizing when someone goes out of his way and validating his extra effort. Genuine praise is one of the most powerful reinforcers we will ever know. This is not blanket praise or praise for nothing, but a true recognition of little things that make the world go around, whether it be toward the woman who empties the garbage can or the guy who cleans the bathrooms.

Sometimes we fail to recognize that the average worker is a lot more important in holding the world together than the executive in the posh office. This may be a difficult skill to use in times of tension because we are tempted to use validation sparingly when we are at odds with another person. However, without it, we move backwards.

One-minute reflection:

The next time you have to deal with an uptight waiter or an edgy clerk, try a few words of validation. "Looks like this place sure is busy today! I admire anyone who can deal with so many people. It seems like a very busy day, but don't worry about us. Take your time. We're not in a hurry."

You will be surprised. Most of the time you will get better service because you noticed and you cared. You may even get a smile. By using genuine validation in difficult times, we can energize others. When people recognize our efforts, it brightens our day and tells us that someone cares and we do matter. And it is such a simple way to demonstrate thoughtfulness and pass the human spirit on to others when we take the time to say, "I care, and you matter."

> As long as the world keeps turning and spinning, we're going to be dizzy, and we're going to make mistakes.
>
> —*Mel Brooks*

Skill #5

A Jerk Whisperer apologizes and can admit to wrongdoings

Apologizing is a powerful tool that makes a monumental personal statement. If ever we reach a point in life at which we find it difficult to admit fault, we will begin to sever many of our connections to others. The most incompatible people on the planet cannot admit to errors, apologize, or ask for forgiveness. They expect you to tough it out. By far, the most difficult people in leadership roles are those who are never wrong and never apologize.

I once worked for a boss who never admitted errors, and even when he was wrong, he never apologized. Even when he made major errors, he could not admit that he had made a mistake. In most cases his ego prompted him to deflect blame to others.

At the time, I worked in a job where people would occasionally pull gags on one another. Two employees, Roger and Andy, were the worst culprits. One day, Roger snuck into Andy's office and sent an email to everyone on the job from his computer: "I quit. I've had enough of you people. Today is my last day. Sincerely, Andy."

We all chuckled because we knew Andy loved his job, and of course, a follow-up email came about ten minutes later saying, "Pay no attention to the last message. Someone was pulling a gag. I am not quitting! Love, Andy!"

A short time later, the boss decided to forward these fun gag emails to his wife. He did this by attaching a note to the two emails as he told his wife, "Nadine, look at these stupid emails from these people. Now can you see what kinds of fools I have to work with in this place?"

You may wonder how I knew that the boss wrote this email to his wife. Believe it or not, everyone on the job knew. Why? Because instead of hitting the send button, he hit the send-to-everyone button. When he realized what he had done, he followed with another email stating, "Please disregard the previous email. It was inadvertently sent."

Yes, of course, the great catch-all for mistakes is to blame your behaviors on "inadvertently." He offered no apology nor admission of wrongdoing. Even in blatant disregard for others' feelings, and in spite of calling his co-workers fools, he would not apologize. I suppose I should give him a break; it was the first time he ever said please! He was hoping that people would disregard the previous email, but in reality, it was not disregarded; it was highly regarded for years to come as one of the funniest things he ever did. As my father would say, "Well, you had it coming."

Too much ego always results in the inability to make oneself resemble a humble human being with normal human feelings. The most anal-retentive people on the planet will never apologize. The reason for that is because an apology would make them vulnerable. It would mean they would have to stop believing in that moment that they are superior to others. The problem is that they do not care, and they desperately need to believe that everyone is beneath them. They live tragic, lonely lives because they isolate themselves on a make-believe cloud where no one exists except themselves. In the end, they die very sad and lonely.

One-minute reflection:

The next time you realize that you have made a mistake and possibly hurt someone's feelings, examine why and how an apology may make life better for both of you. A genuine apology is often one of the biggest leaps forward in any relationship. There are three functions of an apology. First, is the intention to be at peace with your conscience. You are saying, "I need to apologize because I can't live with me." Ask yourself: "Am I happy with who I am right now?" The second function is that you genuinely seek to ease another's pain. Ask yourself: "Can I go through life and think of myself as a person who wants pain for others?" The third function is perhaps the most important—that you apologize because you are saying that the other person truly deserves better than what you did. Ask yourself: "Do people deserve the best me or the worst me?"

Never be afraid to admit that you are a normal person with normal problems and normal mistakes. To be a good Jerk Whisperer, you need to float in harmony on the same cloud as everyone else. A wonderful outcome of apologizing is the respect you will gain from others in the end. William Faulkner once said, "Unless you're ashamed of yourself now and then, you're not honest." When we apologize and admit to wrongdoings, we are much more honest with ourselves.

> No problem is so big or so complicated that it can't be run away from.
> —*Linus (in "Peanuts," by Charles Shulz)*

Skill #6

A Jerk Whisperer can let go and use assertive delay

Forgiveness is the act of letting go. Forgiveness does not mean what you did is okay, or we will be best friends again, or you are absolved of your guilt. The true meaning of forgiveness has to do with not allowing anyone to have power over you. It is saying, "I will no longer allow what you did to have power over me."

Letting go can also mean that we are able to wait. It is not important to act immediately on every impulse. A very powerful tool for communicating, healing, and understanding is the simple act of waiting. We teach children and adults alike to stop and count to ten before reacting to a situation. When tension is high in a conversation, discussion, or meeting, it is important that we calmly ask for another day. Choose a time and place when tension has lowered, and clear thoughts will prevail.

One of the skills found in masterful group facilitators is that they constantly address the process of communication, and they separate it from the content. When people become abusive or irrational, these facilitators stop the conversation and suggest, "Let's set that issue aside and talk about what's going on in here. There is a lot of tension and anger."

The response may be, "I know I'm yelling, but I'm just passionate about this issue, and I have the right to fight for my views!"

The effective facilitator might say, "Yes, I recognize your passion, but you are also being discourteous, and it's entirely possible to talk about this without being disrespectful. You have the right to be passionate, but not the right to be offensive or hurtful." As the old saying goes: the stronger the argument, the less the need to raise one's voice.

One of the problems we make for ourselves is that we want to settle the things right here and now. We know from research that in situations in schools in which tension escalates between a teacher and a student, about 90% of the time, it's the teacher who is escalating. She feels that if she slows down, backs down, or calms down, then she has lost the battle.

It is like trying to put up a tent in a hurricane. It makes no sense. No matter how hard you try, the wind will keep slapping you in the face. It is better to find an appropriate way to delay, or walk away, or wait for another hour, another day, and another moment. It is not a sign of weakness when you lay down your weapons; it is a sign of strength to know when, how, and where to seek a resolution.

Assertive delay is also an efficient use of time. If the conversation or meeting is going nowhere, it is best to try to make it more effective by waiting until tempers have cooled. This holds true for family members, spouses, co-workers, neighbors, and so on. There is a time and a place in which we can achieve maximum effectiveness and say, "Hey, I really sense the tension rising between us, and I think it would be a good idea if we cooled down and got back to this later." It can be as simple as saying, "I'm sorry if I'm adding anything to this. I think too much of our relationship to jeopardize it this way."

Often, when I suggest assertive delay, I hear people say, "Sure, that sounds good in theory, but what if you are in the middle of a crisis and you don't have the luxury of delay?" Crises occur in our lives, but we have to be careful not to turn everything into a crisis. Some people have fifty crises a day. Outside of real war and life and death situations, there are no real crises. If the coffeemaker is a crisis, re-evaluate your life. When a child has a meltdown in a supermarket, it is not a crisis; it is what two-year-olds do when they are tired.

The other excuse I hear is, "Yes, but even if I have assertive delay, they won't respond." In this case, you either have no faith in your skills, or you are simply making a judgment that asserting yourself is a skill for which you feel unprepared. It takes courage, timing, patience, and forethought to develop skills in the art of de-escalation. We just have to be sure that we do not waste our life waiting for the right time to use the skill of assertiveness. If we do not attack our fear of asserting ourselves, we live in a world of self-doubt (I'll never be strong enough), uncertainty (I wonder what tomorrow will bring), and false hope (Maybe things will get better on their own, magically, or maybe they will disappear or turn into someone else's problem).

One-minute reflection:

1. There are a lot of people who will come into our lives and hurt us. Think of one person who occupies a lot of space in your mind because you cannot let go of him. Imagine what life would be like if he no longer held that power over you. Think of life for one day without that burden. At the very least, even if you do not solve the problem, remind yourself of what you value—peaceful relationships—and most importantly, that you are not ready to give up hope. By stating that the relationship is more important than the issue, you are telling the other party that you value him, and you value your future together.

2. If you need to let go physically, try to use a metaphor. Write the person's name on a sheet of paper and throw it away or throw it into a fire—"I am finished with your power over me. I am letting go."—A friend of mine had a novel idea. He would write the name of his jerk on the bottom of his shoe. It was his way of saying, "I'm going to let you wear off of me." It always wore off. He always let go.

> In the end, everything is a gag.
> —Charlie Chaplin

Skill #7
A Jerk Whisperer laughs at him- or herself—daily

One of the greatest strengths of the accomplished Jerk Whisperer is to see his or her own faults and laugh. It is important to laugh at ourselves and to laugh with others. When people fail to laugh at the incongruencies in their lives, they lose their sense of self-appreciation. If you go for a day without laughing at yourself, re-evaluate what you see in the mirror. If you go for a day without laughing with others, re-evaluate your relationships. If you go for a day without laughing at the absurdities in the world, re-evaluate your life.

Take caution to avoid humor at the expense of others; this is true psychopathology. The bullies, the insecure, the mean girls, the gossipers, and the self-persecuted have a distorted need to laugh at others to create a sense of self-elevation on the world's pecking-order. Sometimes it can be a natural response to cliques (generally found in adolescents), but if you have a "mean girls" clique or a mean co-workers clique in your adult life, it is a sign of insecurity, restless obsessions, and a lack of confidence. "I need to do this so I can feel that I am as good or better than they are."

If you know who you are, if you are secure in who you are, and you know your true values, you will always laugh with a healthy sense of humor.

Nothing in this world feels better than a healthy belly laugh with a loved one. A good laugh with others is like a life hug around your relationship. A good laugh at yourself is like a life hug you deserve.

Think about the last time you were around people who laughed for vindictiveness, racism, sexism, or from purely a hateful point of view. I guarantee that you did not feel revitalized when you left them. You probably became more angry and justified in your hate.

Think about the last time you spent an evening with friends and laughed at fun things. Think about a time you laughed yourself silly or you laughed until you nearly lost bladder control. I guarantee that you slept better, and you had more compassion for life.

In the end, laughter is just plain fun, but it also may literally save our lives. It is a miraculous medicine that actually can heal illness. There is research suggesting that people who laugh very little have greater frequencies of illnesses and accidents. It also has been shown that laughter can build our immune systems, change blood-cell counts, balance brain chemistry, and in many cases, heal diseases.

One-minute reflection:

Every day we make a meal of life. How you set your plate to start the day may result in a lovely meal for the rest of the day. In order to laugh every day, we cannot view laughter as the goal itself, but we need to understand that laughter is the evidence that we have a readiness to find joy in all things.

Your goal has to be to set the plate with openness, an ability to slow down, and an expectation that you will embrace the chaos of the day rather than fight it. It is more than having a sense *of* humor; it is a matter of having a sense *for* humor. Take a deep breath when you expect chaos, and look for the natural humor in things. Soon you will find that you are a natural magnet for others' positive energy. There is nothing more fun than being around an accomplished laugher. Most of the incongruencies in life are naturally funny. Let kids be kids, let the hurriers be hurriers, let the busy life be a sign that you are full of life, and let the muddy paws on the dog be a sign that you can enjoy the dog just being a dog.

What the heck, laugh it up; live longer! Laughter—practice it daily.

> A loving person lives in a loving world. A hostile person lives in a hostile world: everyone you meet is your mirror.
>
> —*Ken Keyes, Jr.*

Skill #8

A Jerk Whisperer mentally rehearses rational scenarios

One of the most debilitating habits that a person can have is to be upset and channel the pain into mental rehearsals of vengeful, spiteful, or hostile outcomes. Did you ever have a tense verbal exchange with a driver, or a clerk, or a co-worker, or a boss, then obsess about telling him off? Or running him off the road? Or screaming at him? Or just plain, "Giving him a piece of my mind!"

Ask yourself, "What's the point? What was the usefulness in that scenario running through my brain? Did it make me calmer? More serene? More loving? Did it make me a better friend, spouse, parent?"

If you are upset about something in the past, drop it. Instead of obsessing, "I should have given her a piece of my mind! I should have told her off! I should have put him in his place!" perhaps find some solace in the fact that you did not act contrary to your values. Be proud, not spiteful.

If you are worried, concerned, or interested in some upcoming event in the future, rehearse rational outcomes. It does not make you a better person to think: "If she says this… then I will counter it with a better attack!"

If you have an upcoming meeting or conversation, rehearse rational outcomes. What do you hope will happen? What would be a best-case scenario? People who mentally rehearse bad future scenarios are dooming their lives in the interim. They live a life consumed with futile battles with things they cannot change to begin with. "Sure, it might be tense in this discussion, but then again, maybe I can use my power to make it better than it might have been."

I have worked with people who reflect on nearly every meeting by saying, "I was really dreading today's meeting. That went better than I thought it would. I had worried about that meeting for the past two days!" What worries me about these people is that they say this several times a week. It is as though their brains are incapable of rehearsing rational and positive scenarios, and they have a constant expectation that this is going to be bad. "This is going to be stressful. I just know it's going to be horrible." In all of that time leading up to the meeting, they are losing their hair and losing their minds as they persistently choose to have thoughts that reduce the quality of their life. Why not rehearse positive outcomes and deal with the negatives as they come along? Positive mental rehearsals allow us to practice success. Negative rehearsals only allow us to practice losses, defeats, and painful scenarios. We know from research in psychological kinesiology that athletes who rehearse winning tend to perform better. Those who fear that they may miss a shot in a basketball game or dread the thought of striking out in a baseball game increase their chances for these errors. What keeps us from doing the same in our relationships? If we need to talk to a loved one about a situation, why do we rehearse tension when it has not occurred? Why do we view the upcoming meeting with miserable anticipation? It is as though we would rather believe that it is going to go bad and be right about it instead of believing that it may turn out well and take our chances.

Have you ever been in a no-win situation, and you were accompanied by an optimist? Is it not wonderful? Yes, we may miss the plane, but we will make the best of it! There is no situation in which the optimist is not seeking a lesson.

> There is a proven way to keep the hurt that comes
> from relationships to a minimum, and that is to train
> ourselves to become good at being with others.
>
> —*P.M. Forni*

In the context of our own lives, we mentally need to rehearse scenes of positive outcomes, and as we do, we reenergize our spirits. We need to make it a habit to see the best in the future and see the positive in the face of seemingly insurmountable conditions. In the wonderful book *Choosing Civility*, P. M. Forni pointed out that we need to work on what he called *behavioral literacy.* As he says in the quote above, we need to train ourselves and others to be competent in being with others. When we work on this training, it becomes an exciting endeavor to renew our quests for civility.

It can be as simple as connecting with someone by confirming the obvious. Even when you need to give critical feedback, ask yourself, "What decent quality have I seen in this person?" Miserable people always forward their negative critique of things before the positive. It is as though they believe that they own the corner of the market on reality. It does not matter whether you are talking about a book, movie, or person, miserable people can find a fault!

John Wooden, the legendary UCLA basketball coach, often talked about using a positive/critical/positive sandwich when offering critical feedback. He suggests that if we verbalize a positive trait, followed by the critical feedback, and then close our statement with another positive trait, people are more apt to listen and remember what we said. If all we give others is critical feedback, we discourage them. If we can emphasize the positive, we encourage others. All it takes is developing the knack of seeing the good and mentioning it. Miserable people will complain, "I don't have time! I need to get to the issue!" It is not that you don't have time; it is more of a matter of not having the aptitude to see the positive in others. I am convinced that people would rather see the good in the world, but they get caught in social traps.

I released a DVD titled *The Five Golden Rules for Staying Connected to Children*. Some of the rules include "Practice the Behaviors You Would Like to See in Others," "Be a Guide—Not a Dictator," "Become a Scientist, Not a Victimist." I hand out a lot of those DVDs to people. I give a lot of them away, and often I hand them out to my students and simply say, "What's the sixth golden rule?" I urge them to have an original thought on the subject—What do you do to remind yourself about how to treat others?

The responses are often amazing, with simple words, sayings, or maybe a slant on something they heard people say, like: size people up instead of sizing them down; every day has a defining moment—it is our duty to find it and make the most of it; remember to have child expectations for a child—not adult expectations for a child; treat our enemies with the greatest of kindness—they need it the most; be a dream chaser—not a dream taker; instead of seeing a secretary, clerk, student, or waitress, see a person; notice people; say thanks for every little thing!

I am convinced that the majority of people want to be positive, rational thinkers, but we fall into the negative traps because it is easier; it takes no effort—only a cynical mind. Not seeing the positive allows us to shield ourselves by not making us appear to be compassionate and vulnerable.

We can do things right by turning confrontations not into battles, but into decisions. If we are doing things we will regret later, we lack restraint. If we continue to go through life without change, we lack wisdom. If we cannot think of a better way to do things, we lack vision. Sometimes it can also be a simple matter of understanding. We treasure the things we understand the most. When you understand something as important as love, you treasure it more.

One-minute reflection:

The next time you find yourself in the middle of a stress-filled day, stop doing whatever you are doing, and find a quiet place with no distractions, no sound, no cellphones, radios, televisions, or computer screens. Simply stop for a moment to be alone with your thoughts. Take one moment to reflect on how you may be obsessing. The key is not to revisit the obsession—"My boss is making my life crazy!" Rather, examine how you are obsessing.

First, ask yourself: How long? Have I been thinking about this all night long? All morning? All week?

Second, ask yourself: What is my intention? Do I really want to solve this? Or do I just need to win? Be right? Get even?

Third, ask yourself: Right now, in this moment of my internal tirade, if I could choose an alternative emotion, what would it be? Would I rather be calm? Would I rather find serenity?

Most often, if we do a quick analysis of the obsession, we find that the only thing in our way is our ego, and that ego is crushing the life out of our day. That unsolved need in our head is not being solved. We are certain that we need to obsess over a victorious outcome, a tirade-laced outcome, or a "you need to feel my pain" outcome, rather than a peaceful one.

Sometimes that path to a peaceful set of thoughts is the simple realization that it is a war that will no longer exist if you simply choose not to fight it.

Rehearse a rational scenario, a positive outcome, and a happy ending. Even if it does not come out that way, you will be a lot happier in the interim. Most importantly, you will increase your chances for a positive outcome. There is enough real misery in the world. Life's too short to waste it on imagined misery.

> The longer I live, the more beautiful life becomes.
> —Frank Lloyd Wright

Skill #9

A Jerk Whisperer can state at least one thing each day for which he or she is grateful

Throughout history, we are aware of philosophers, psychologists, and counselors who emphasized the power of our thoughts. Most of the time, these suggestions about the way we think attempt to correct the thoughts that trouble us. From ancient philosophers to modern-day self-help, we can point to our thoughts as the promoters of fulfillment. Our thinking is clearly a precursor to our emotions. We feel something in connection to what we are thinking.

Many of the things for which we are grateful will appear in our thoughts at various times in our experiences. When gas prices go up, we may tend to treasure travel because it can no longer be taken for granted. We also may feel grateful for a loved one when he or she does something nice for us or simply kisses us good night at bedtime. These emotions may hold true for food, clothes, and other small blessings. On a more personal note, we are grateful for love when we realize how important it is in our lives. When we experience the death of someone close to us, it can cause us to appreciate life more than before.

If we fill our daily thoughts with the things we perceive to be deficits, we will feel incomplete. "I need to get this possession. I need to win this argument. I need my day to fit exactly into this schedule. I need others to appreciate me. I need to arrive at this exact time."

Instead of these negative habits of thinking, when we fill our thoughts with experiences of gratefulness for needs that have been met, we feel complete. We feel whole.

Researchers have confirmed many things that our common sense already knows to be true. As we shape our thoughts, we shape our day. When the alarm goes off, does your brain immediately go to the unmet needs? The unmet tasks? "Oh goodness! It's Tuesday. I've got to get moving early today! Work is piling up at the office! The highways will be a mess! Oh my, the kids need to get on the bus! Oh gads, I think we are out of cereal. What will we eat?"

Would your day be different if it went this way? Alarm goes off... "Ah Tuesday... (deep, long breath...). I sure am thankful I have a job. I cannot imagine what it would be like to wake up everyday and wonder how I am going to feed my family. I need to wake the kids. I am so thankful for their health. I cannot imagine what our house will be like one day when I no longer hear the pitter patter of their little feet around here. Goodness! We are out of cereal. Let me see...I think there is some oatmeal or toast, or I can pick up something on the way. Look at those kids sleeping. There are 400 million children in the world right now who are starving. I feel so grateful. I am so fortunate."

Research in positive psychology has suggested that if we take a single minute to start our day by thinking about things for which we are grateful, we can change our blood pressure, improve our immune system, be safer on the road, and have more satisfactory relationships.

I find this quite amazing! You do not need a health insurance plan to get it done! It costs less than pills, therapy, or a fancy mood ring! Our thoughts change the chemistry of our brains. Many people already know this, as they do it with meditation, yoga, or prayer. Contentment and effective interaction with our environment have less to do with the food on the plate than they do with how you set the table.

When we set up our day with thoughts that provoke tension, resentment, neediness, and perfectionism, we are instantly doomed. When we start the day with appreciation, we also set the table for a virtual feast for the rest of the day.

One-minute reflection:

If you are struggling with what to think about, try this: for the next week, be very diligent with a pattern of thinking. (Oh no. I can hear your thoughts. Please do not sigh; it will only take one minute per day.) Before you leave your bed, think of these three things:

1. Someone I love right now is…

2. Something I have, or something that happened to me for which I feel grateful, is…

3. Something good I believe will happen to me in the future is…

After you have done this for a week, try to think of these three things before you go to sleep as well. Researchers also suggest we sleep better when we create positive thoughts before we doze off. The result of better sleep? Less stress, less fidgeting, better concentration, fewer accidents, and fewer illnesses. And it costs less than fancy psychoanalysis and sleeping pills!

This strategy is extremely important for the effective Jerk Whisperer because we do not want to set ourselves up for crabby episodes that lead to being a Crabby Jerk.

When you end your day, ask yourself what the best part of it was? If you have survived another day, it is a success. If someone loved you today, it was a robust day. If you made someone happy, if you comforted someone, if you made someone laugh, it was a wonderful day!

How do you measure a successful day? A rule of thumb is this: never evaluate your personal success by anything that can be measured. If your life is measured by possessions, gold medals, or dollars, you may end up with a lot of pretty stuff. You also may have to learn how to enjoy it alone.

The best part of my day is not when I get in the last word or win an argument. It is when I hold my wife in my arms, and I am thankful that she is safely home from work, and I am thankful that she loves me in spite of all my neurotic ways. That is the best part of my day.

> If you have made another person on this earth smile, your life has been worthwhile.
> —*Sr. Mary Christelle Macaluso*

Skill #10
A Jerk Whisperer gives away all of the things he or she can make from nothing

When you strip away all the glitz, glamour, gadgets, possessions, and accessories, what is life?

There are many examples in history when human beings applied themselves to great causes. These moments represent an evolution in character. One such example was from World War II when millions of people were terrorized, beaten down, and executed by a truly psychopathological force led by a man named Adolf Hitler. As millions of Jews were forced into Nazi death camps, they had to endure horrors that most people cannot even imagine.

In the profoundly moving book *Man's Search for Meaning*, Viktor Frankl recollected his life in the notorious Auschwitz Nazi death camp. Frankl was one of millions who lost everything except for the bodies they occupied. Many of us cannot imagine going for a day without our cellphones, let alone our homes, plasma televisions, computers, cars, food, or loved ones.

There was an incident in this camp when a man had stolen some potatoes from the food supply, and the Nazi guards did not know who had done it. The guards told the inmates to give up the man who had stolen the potatoes or the entire compound would not eat for a day.

Even though many prisoners knew who had stolen the potatoes, all 2,500 men chose to starve for one day. They would not let the larger evil win the battle by forcing them to turn on another human being who would surely be hanged for his error in judgment. Not only was it extraordinary that this solidarity could occur, it was also a monumental collective gesture of forgiveness. What followed was even more remarkable. That evening, as the starving men talked about many situations in which it seemed that life could never get worse—hangings for small crimes, starvation, torture, and random executions—the conversation turned to hope. That evening, the discussion turned darkness to brightness as the men talked about the things that no one can take away. Those things had to do with life's meaning. The most meaningful things in life are the things that can be created from nothing. They are also the things that no one can take away from us—things such as pride, love, hope, faith, and choices. Often, the simple but fundamental difference between surviving and dying is not food, water, or disease. Frankl reminded us that those who retain hope are the ones who are more likely to survive.

On 9/11 when the World Trade Towers were struck down in another act of psychopathology, I was living in Albany, New York. I was grading papers for a graduate course I was teaching at the college. One of the hijacked planes flew directly overhead on that awful morning. Having spent time in New York City, it was especially traumatic to think about the decent people who were victims on that horrible day. I had a chance later to talk to a principal from a school in downtown Manhattan. She had to be the one to tell many children that their parents would not be coming home that night.

Despite the thousands of stories of horror and heartbreak, what followed was a testimony to what we really know about the nature of humanity. There was indeed anger, fear, and even some hatred. Largely, however, amongst those involved, the spirit and energy that followed was not a desire for retribution, vindication, or punishment. What followed were decent people holding one another, caring for one another, loving one another, and trying to do anything in their power to heal one another.

Unfortunately, before our lives are over, there is probably a good chance that we will experience more atrocities. We have to choose a path, and we have to be prepared to choose a path. We start by doing this on a day-to-day basis as we respond to challenging moments of incivility, no matter how large or how small they may be. I would like to hope that we could care for one another and strive for this revolution of character all the time, not just when we have to endure the large-scale, horrible events.

If you choose this path, you need to be prepared to be seen as naïve. People may ask, "How can you be so naïve to talk of the world as though it is still overflowing with love? How naïve, how shallow, how narrow it is for you to think that this world can improve? How can you be so stupid?" I may be naïve, but at least I am sure of what it does for me. Perhaps narrow, focused, and naïve is my goal, because when love is no longer my goal, I lose my power of devotion, my power to care, power to heal, and power to hope. If I join the hostile and the pessimistic, that is all I will ever see in the world and all I will ever see in others. If I am angry, then hostility is all I can build in others, promote in others, and teach others. I would rather stay focused on the kind of world we deserve and the kind of world our children deserve.

In the end, it is the things that no one can take from us that really matter. In the end, it is goodness that prevails. For all the intangibles that we debate, one thing is eminently clear: Love is a miracle. What makes it a miracle is that any one of us can create an abundance of it from nothing. We can give it all away and still have just as much as when we started. Make it a habit to give away all the things you can make from nothing. Give away all your love. Do not hoard it. Give away all your kindness. Do not hold back. Give away all your hope. Life is short.

On any given day, you can find a funeral where people are standing around and talking about the things they wish they had given away yesterday. Notice they are not saying, "I wish I had one more opportunity to give him a boat. I wish I had one more opportunity to give her flowers or a new cellphone." They are saying, "I wish I had one more opportunity to give her my arms—to tell her how much I love her."

We need to get busy today. There is no better day than today to tell others how much we love them and to treat others with the decency they deserve.

The miracle is that it does not take money, possessions, or fame to change another human being. All it takes is a will to make a difference. All it takes is a will to build instead of destroy. All it takes is a will to comfort others rather than hurt. Isn't it exciting to think that you could create a miracle every day of your life?

To you, the reader, I would like to conclude by sending you my best wishes for a wondrous and joyful future. Whether you find agreement or disagreement in what I have written, you have read this far, and that is evidence alone of your optimism. You have something wonderful to share with millions of other humans, and that thing is love, and it is powered by hope. These are the things we can never afford to lose, and they are by far the most valuable things that humanity can ever possess. Each day you can create a better world. Each day you can create new miracles, even if they are small ones.

When you picked up this book, you were interested in finding some techniques or skills for dealing with the hostility in the world. You recognized that this tension is ineffective and unproductive, and you wanted change. Being a Jerk Whisperer is less about taming the beasts in the world and more about taming struggles within our hearts. If you are striving to make the world a more peaceful place, you already have done it. If you continue to do it, your life will always have purpose. I hope you will always cling to this simple truth: Any act in the name of love always will be worth the effort. Any life lived in the name of love will be meaningful.

Final reflection:

What am I willing to do to get busy today? (The question only takes three seconds to ask but can be answered over your lifetime.)

Dedication

Nick Birchak
1984-2011

Is it a crisis or an inconvenience?

The following is an excerpt of a presentation from the 2010 American College Personnel Association national conference in Boston, Massachusetts.

Nick Birchak, co-presenting a workshop on how to become a Jerk Whisperer:

"One of the best things we can do for ourselves is to know the difference between a crisis and an inconvenience. Hurricane Katrina was a crisis; 9/11 was a crisis; a loved one dying of cancer is a crisis. For your information, however, long lines at the coffee shop? Not a crisis! Traffic jams on the way to work? Not a crisis! My computer program isn't working? Not a crisis! If you have more than one crisis a month, you need to re-evaluate your life! I've got news for you: most of life's

struggles are inconveniences. But if you wake up every day and make the traffic, email, weather, dishes in the sink, or the dog's muddy paws into a crisis, you are going to live an incredibly miserable life. For me, I rarely have a crisis; there's already enough in the world. If you make everything into a crisis, something else happens to you: you start to see more of the negativity in the world. You look for more of the bad qualities in people and more of the disappointments in your average day. The most beautiful thing about life is that it doesn't have to be that way. We can train ourselves to wake up every day and tell ourselves, "There will be no crises today." It's that simple. Most crises are in our heads, not in the real world. When you remove the imaginary crises from your life, you will find that you have a lot more time to give away your smiles, give away your hugs, see the best in others, solve problems, and relieve a little bit of the suffering in the world.

I had the honor of co-presenting workshops with Nick Birchak on eight different occasions. We presented to teachers, state workers, undergraduate students, graduate students, college administrators, and at the national ACPA conference. During the writing of this book, Nick suffered a massive epileptic seizure and died in his sleep. He was twenty-seven years old, and he was my son. For our family (Annie—mother, and Brandon—younger brother, and myself), it was the worst day of our lives. The world lost an amazing human being, and we, the Birchak family, lost a part of our soul.

Nick lived a more difficult life than most of us. He was legally blind, and beyond an inch, everything was a blur, yet it was obvious to most of us that he saw the world a lot better than we did. He suffered from joint problems, eyesight difficulties, and epilepsy, and he endured more than twenty surgeries in his short life. In spite of all his struggles, he never complained and never failed to smile and laugh each day of his life. His sense of humor was contagious, and if you spent enough time around him, you could count on occasionally being crippled by bouts of laughter. Nick was the most grateful person I have ever known. In spite of his challenges, he did a lot of amazing things in his life, including earning a bachelor's and a master's degree. He became a specialist in computer programs for people with disabilities. He won awards in Lindy Hop swing dancing, wrestling, and weightlifting (including an AAU bench press record that has remained unbroken as of this writing). He was given awards by the governor and the attorney general for his character.

When we presented workshops together, Nick would talk about the difference between a crisis and an inconvenience. As Nick talked about these things, he would become very animated, and audiences could always see his passion for the possible. His dream was that if we give away all of our smiles, hugs, and compassion, perhaps our love will continue to be around even after we are gone. His dream is now our reality. His love is still around, and I'm proud to carry his message in this book. He was my greatest teacher for turning my everyday imagined crises into mere inconveniences.

For that reason and many others, this book, in its entirety, is dedicated to the memory of Nick.

The world became a little better place because of his years in it. My challenge to you, the reader, is to try to live for one day without a complaint. Try to go for one day without gossip or a disparaging word about others. Try to live for one day without an imagined crisis. You will find that you have a lot more time to love others, open doors for others, and exercise patience in an impatient world. You will notice that this way of life will relieve a lot of suffering (including your own). You also will discover what it was like to live like Nick. He had the courage to live like that for twenty-seven years.

References

Forni, P. M. (2002). *Choosing Civility*. New York: St. Martin's Press.

Frankl, V. E. (1997). *Man's Search for Meaning: An introduction to logotherapy*. New York: Pocket Books.

About the Author

Dr. Stephen Birchak is a professor, speaker, father, husband, and reformed class clown. He is an internationally acclaimed speaker and motivates thousands of people each year. He is also the author of *The Champions of Dignity* and *How to Build a Child's Character—By Tapping into Your Own*. Stephen Birchak has a doctorate in Education from the University of Northern Colorado, a Master of Arts in Community Counseling from Adams State College, and a Bachelor of Arts in Health Education from the University of Northern Colorado. He has been a professor and administrator in higher education for more than thirty years. He lives in upstate New York and teaches at The College of Saint Rose in Albany.